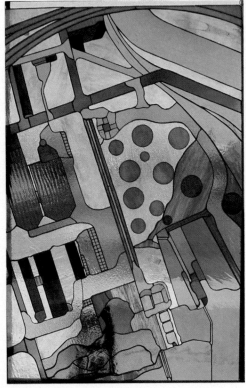

C-2.

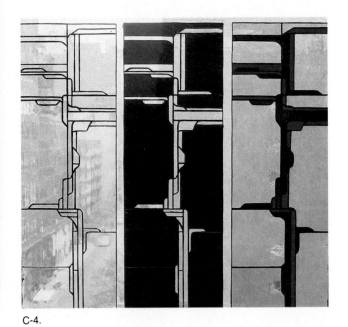

C-4.

C-3.

C-5.

C-6.

C-7.

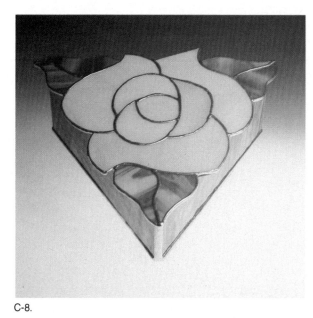

C-8.

C-10.

C-9.

C-11.

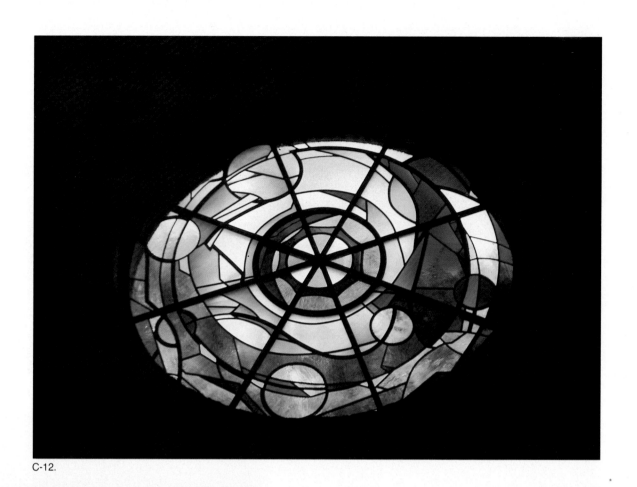

C-12.

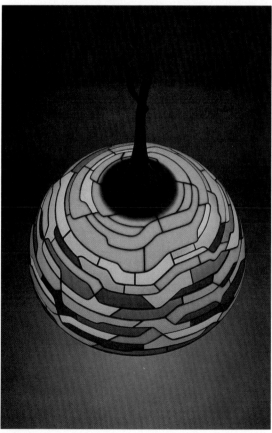

C-13.

C-14.

C-15.

C-17.

C-16.

DESIGN FOR STAINED GLASS

DESIGN FOR STAINED GLASS

JENNIE FRENCH

VAN NOSTRAND REINHOLD COMPANY
New York Cincinnati Toronto London Melbourne

"The mastery of great things comes with the doing of trifles."

Henry Miller, *The Colossus of Maroussi* (1941)

First published in paperback in 1983
Copyright © 1979 by Jennie French
Library of Congress Catalog Card Number 78-18001
ISBN 0-442-22449-4

Printed in the United States of America
Designed by Loudan Enterprises

Van Nostrand Reinhold Company Inc.
135 West 50th Street, New York, NY 10020

Van Nostrand Reinhold Publishers
1410 Birchmount Road
Scarborough, Ontario M1P 2E7, Canada

Van Nostrand Reinhold Australia Pty. Ltd.
480 Latrobe Street
Melbourne, Victoria 3000, Australia

Van Nostrand Reinhold Company Limited
Molly Millars Lane
Wokingham, Berkshire, England RG11 2PY

Cloth edition published 1979 by Van Nostrand Reinhold Company

16   15   14   13   12   11   10   9   8   7   6   5   4   3   2

CONTENTS

ACKNOWLEDGMENTS

I would like to thank my friends for their support, especially R. Stitely, Mrs. Cover, Kasov, and Edge; the contributing stained glass artists; and the graphic and fine arts contributors not included in the biographies: Mike Cardea, Olivia DeBerardinis, Anthony Downes, Laura Kiaulénas, Alma Kline, Mike Revere, and Alice Scarborough. I would also like to thank Phil Koenig and Phil Mazzurco for their consultation on the photography section, and Ron Bly for typing the original manuscript.

Many thanks to:

Two of my mentors, Susan Greenbaum—who is a major influence in this book and my art in general—for her assistance with the craft section and Tom Venturella for his help and encouragement; Lori Sanchez for modeling;

My editor, Leslie Wenger, for all her patience and work; Rose Vasquez for her work on this and the first book;

My family, especially Mother, for all she does just as a matter of course, and Ellen Sanchez just because.

All photographs and line drawings are by the author unless credited otherwise.

COLOR PLATES

C-1
Furman, *Shutters* (1977). This detail of a free-standing sculpture shows some of the delicate metal construction work that occurs in the design. The sculpture, mounted in a heavy steel frame measuring 33″ × 18″ (83.8cm × 45.7cm) is from the collection of Glass Masters Guild in New York City. (Photo by John B. Young Jr. and French)

C-2
Garber. The rectangular panel is an abstracted aerial view of the New Haven, Connecticut harbor and measures 35″ × 54″ (88.9cm × 137.2cm). The circles are epoxied unto the glass. (Photo by Garber)

C-3
Baum and Gelband (1977). The mural measures 12′ × 4 1/2′ (3.6m × 11.35m) and is installed in the Old Mill Inn in Spring Lake Heights, New Jersey. It contains approximately eight thousand pieces and was designed and fabricated by the designers themselves. (Photo by French)

C-4
Greenbaum, *Trilogy* (1977). Each panel measures 10″ × 28 1/2″ (25.4cm × 72.4cm) and remains in the collection of the artist. It is important to notice how different each panel appears, although cut from the same pattern, due to the color selection. (Photo by French)

C-5
Greenbaum. The lamp measures 18″ (45.7cm) in diameter and hangs in the Harris residence in New York City. Many of the nearly one-thousand pieces are smaller than a dime and it took approximately three weeks from conception to completion. The lamp is a nonrepeating design. (Photo by French)

C-6
Sell (1977). The fish measures 43″ × 24″ × 23″ (109cm × 61cm × 58.4cm). It is a lighted sculpture rather than a hanging lamp and is fabricated with copperfoil. (Photo by Nancy Lewis)

C-7
Venturella, *Tribute to Georgia O'Keefe* (1977). The two windows are installed in the Busel residence, Chicago, Illinois. Each leaded window measures 26″ × 46″ (66cm × 116.8cm), mounted with a 2″ (5.1cm) space between them. (Photos by Larry Pyrzynski)

C-8
Nugget and Nugget (1978). The box is part of the Nuggets' regular commercial line of glasswork. The decorative lid is angled (difficult to see in the picture) to allow it to be seen at all times rather than just when the viewer is directly above it. (Photo by Nugget)

C-9
Avidon (1977). La Folie Restaurant in New York City. The wall mural is approximately 35′ × 7′ (10.5m × 2.1m) and was fabricated at The Greenland Studio. (Photo by French)

C-10
French (1978). The abstract panel measures 16″ × 20″ (40.6cm × 50.8cm) and remains in the collection of the artist. It is indicative of present work. (Photo by French)

C-11
Bakst (1978). These leaded sliding doors are installed in the Cody residence in Brooklyn Heights, New York. Each panel measures 32″ × 34″ (81cm × 86.4cm). The original etched Victorian glass was removed from the doors and sections of it were used in the new panels. (Photo by Bakst)

C-12
Hyams (1978). Maple Knoll Village Chapel in Springdale, Ohio. Shown is one of two rose windows from this commission measuring 6′ (1.8m) in diameter. Not shown are the twenty-two side windows, each measuring 2 1/2′ (.75m) square. All windows were fabricated at The Greenland Studio in New York City, and are excellent examples of how to stretch the limits of the medium. (Photos by Charles Shimel)

C-13
Cushen (1977). The dome lamp is 16″ (40.6cm) across the bottom diameter and is fabricated with copperfoil. The pieces were cut from antique glass, sandblasted, and then shaped with heat to conform to the dome shape. The major problem in construction was the tendency for the long strips of glass to twist during the heating process, much in the way a burning paper match will twist. The pattern is nonrepeating. (Photo by French).

C-14
Cullenbine, *Bears in the Stream*, detail. (Photo by Cullenbine)

C-15
Myers, *Australian Owl Finches*. The panel is installed in a Lake Tahoe residence. The birds were fired three times: umber matt for breast color, trace black matt for the center indentations and rounding of the bodies, and trace black painting for black feathers on heads, breasts, and tails. They are depicted in their natural habitat, in the brush, close to the ground. (Photo by Myers)

C-16
Mellen. The dragons are fabricated in lead came, steel, and polyester. They are installed in the Gelman residence, Englewood, New Jersey, and measure 3′ × 5′ (.9m × 1.5m). They represent the first work in stained glass by Mellen. (Photo by Jennifer Djerks)

C-17
Wilkinson. The 3′ (.9m) rose window is fabricated with copperfoil and framed in wood. It was adapted from a metal buckle from the 1930s and remains in the collection of the artist. (Photo by French)

CONTRIBUTING
STAINED GLASS ARTISTS

Richard Avidon, New York, NY

As well as teaching art and stained glass since 1961, Richard Avidon has exhibited extensively and had his work reproduced in several magazines and a book. He has worked for Rambusch Decorating Co., New York City, and was the design director for the restoration and installation of windows from the 14th century Church of St. Leonhard, Latvanthal, Austria. These windows are on permanent display at the Cloisters, a division of the Metropolitan Museum of Art in New York City. Until recently, he was the New York City correspondent for *Glass* magazine. In his own words, "my work attempts to shape the inner emotional space of the individual and on an architectural scale to reshape perceptions of physical space itself."

Marni Bakst, New York, NY

After attending the University of Chicago and receiving her B.F.A. in graphic design from California College of Arts and Crafts, Marni Bakst studied at the Peter Mollica Studio in Berkeley, California. She then returned to the East and apprenticed at The Greenland Studio in New York City. She has exhibited in several galleries and juried shows in the eastern area and is now working on private commissions and in conjunction with architects.

Stacy Baum, New York, NY

Stacy Baum attended Cooper Union as a painting major. She learned the basics of stained glass work from Chester Gelband and then perfected the craft through trial and error. During the last few years she ran a stained glass business but has now closed the studio in favor of working on private commissions in collaboration with Chester Gelband. Her work is influenced by "the idea of filling space in a beautiful way."

Carole Woody Cullenbine, Palo Alto, CA

Carole Cullenbine is an accomplished designer/instructor with many years' experience in teaching stained glass, decorating, macramé, weaving, and silversmithing. She is the author of a book on mirror designs, *Stained Glass Reflections*, and has other designs appearing in *Window Art*. She is also the author of two books on dollhouse miniatures. Her mirrors, windows, and lamps are especially notable for her realistic use of colors and shapes to capture animals, birds, and plants in glass. At present she is specializing in skylights, room dividers, and door and wall inserts.

Jack Cushen, New York, NY

Since 1955 when he apprenticed to The Robert M. Metcalf Studios in Ohio as a glass painter, Jack Cushen has been actively working with stained glass. His long list of credits include many group and one-man shows, a Benesco first prize award, and various teaching positions on the college level. His work has been published in several books. Until recently, he was a master craftsman at The Greenland Studio and is now working and teaching independently.

Jim Furman, Trumansburg, NY

Jim Furman started out in glass by salvaging two small, wrecked church windows that he discovered in a country antique store draped over and conformed to the shape of an old Coca-Cola machine. He used a partially destroyed 1940 copy of a book on stained glass craft to restore one window and redesign the other. Now, ten years later, he has taught at Cornell University Craft Studios, and Corning Culture Center, and has been an assistant instructor at Haystack Mountain School. He has exhibited at the Ithaca Crafts Fair and the Corning Museum of Glass. His designs often combine heavy copper rods, steel frames, and plumbing sheet metal to form powerful three-dimensional glass sculptures.

Albert J. Garber, New Haven, CT

Al Garber has been working in glass since 1968 without formal technical or design training. He maintains a studio where he works mainly on private commissions.

Chester Gelband, New York, NY

Chester Gelband worked as a cabinetmaker and in wood sculpture before becoming involved with glass. He recently dissolved a studio in which he was part owner that combined workroom, store, and classroom for over one-hundred students a year. He is now working on private commissions in collaboration with Stacy Baum.

Susan Greenbaum, New York, NY

In 1965 there were no women working as craftsmen in a New York City studio and possibly throughout the country except for Susan Greenbaum. At age nineteen she served her apprenticeship at The Greenland Studio under the supervision of Mel Greenland and Jim Hicks. She gained a reputation as one of the best cutters in the trade and became skilled in all aspects of the craft on a professional level, including: leading, copperfoil, epoxy, restoration, and installation. Her independent work now encompasses private commissions, restoring Tiffany lamps, plus designing and selling her own Tiffany-style lamps. She has exhibited in the East and conducted stained-glass classes for children at the Cloisters through the Metropolitan Museum of Art in New York City.

Harriet Hyams, Teaneck, NJ

Eleven years ago Harriet Hyams turned her interest from heavy sculpture in stone, metal, and wood to working with stained glass. Her work reflects the powerful lines and movement gained through years of sculpture and is strongly influenced by Cubism. During the past eleven years she has raised a family, acquired an M.A., had twelve one-man shows, taught art at Columbia College in New York City, and designed a long list of windows for private residences and public and religious buildings.

Barbara Mellen, Carrboro, NC

Combined interest in art and biology have influenced Barbara Mellen in her glass work and design in general. She graduated from The New College in Sarasota, Florida, as a fine arts/illustration major in 1974. Her first workshop was at home in a garage in Massachusetts. She then moved to Nashville, Tennessee, where she spent three years working in a tiny, cramped space, which she feels may have influenced the scale of her pieces. While in Tennessee, she had four one-man shows of glass, ink, and other media. She also visited France specifically to see the windows of the great cathedrals. Recently having moved to North Carolina, she has a sizable studio where she does all of her own work from designing to clean-up afterwards.

Jean Myers, San Francisco, CA

After years of working in watercolor, Jean Myers apprenticed in stained glass under Narcissus Quagliata. Later she studied with Herr Ludwig Schaffrath and most recently with Maureen McGuire. Her feelings about glass are best explained in her own words. "I thoroughly enjoy working on commissions. I do not, in any way, feel that I'm being deprived of my self expression by creating for others, or that I'm losing a thing of beauty when I deliver a window into the buyer's hands. My life is vastly expanded by the search for emotional beauty in my clients' lives and by sharing with them the expression of that beauty in glass." Her delicate sense of design is reinforced by a meticulous attention to craftwork, which often incorporates painting, staining, and etching of glass.

Audry and Michael Nugget, New York, NY

The Nuggets have been working in glass for the past few years and selling to a market that is often occupied by the less talented—department stores and boutiques. Michael Nugget designs and Audry fabricates their moderately priced, high-quality line of commercial glass works. They turned their hobby into a profession when they had a child and decided to work at home rather than pursue their separate careers. Young Alexander Nugget and the business are both alive and thriving!

George Sell, New York, NY

George Sell received a B.F.A. in sculpture and painting from the University of Connecticut in 1966 and an M.F.A. degree in sculpture from Bowling Green University in 1968. His credits include an assistant professorship at the Oswego College of New York from 1969–1975 and numerous exhibitions, one-man shows, and awards for his work. Although he is an all-around artist dedicated to the arts and teaching, he has been deeply involved with stained glass for several years and brings to his work an intimate knowledge of three-dimensional space.

Tom Venturella, New York, NY

A "painter by birth" Tom Venturella found his way into glass as simply another language of art. After graduating from the Art Institute of Chicago in 1969, he moved to New York City and worked at The Greenland Studio. Later he had the privilege of collaborating with the reknowned artist, Benoit Gilsoul, on The Christ Over the City window at St. Johns Capucian Monastery in Madison, New Jersey. The collaboration also resulted in studies and execution of tapestries and sculpture as well as stained glass. On occasion he has been invited back to The Greenland Studio for restoration work on Tiffany lamps and windows, and to fabricate other artist's designs, such as his recent work on The Maple Knoll Village Chapel windows for Harriet Hyams.

Rachel Wilkinson, New York, NY

Born in North Carolina, Rachel Wilkinson has spent the past few years constructing stained glass pieces in her Manhattan studio. In 1973 she studied at The Stained Glass Workshop, Inc., in New York City, then rented a studio space to test her ability and talent by making a six-foot panel. She was so enthused by the results that she quit her job as a researcher for WCBS-TV to pursue a career in stained glass. Her work has been exhibited in the New York area and she now works through private commissions.

INTRODUCTION

This book is an introduction to designing for stained glass. It is directed to those people who have mastered the basic skills of glassworking but who have little or no formal art training. It is the book that I wanted when I first started out.

The world of stained glass has changed dramatically since I first learned the basic skills of the craft. There now exists a bounty of tools, materials, gallery shows, courses, and books hitherto unavailable. Stained glass is also now one of the top five favorite American crafts (and 60/40 solder has more than quadrupled in price). Considering this fact, the absence of information on how to approach glass designing is curious. The subject is not difficult to grasp nor does a special guild stand guard over sacred secrets; yet, the void persists.

There are many ways to get around the old "I can't draw a straight line" syndrome that keeps one chained to pattern books, and it really is more enjoyable to fabricate your own designs. However, since everyone does learn by imitation and repetition, eighty-four fairly complex designs have been included in Chapter 2 for your study and practice. The term complex does not mean that the individual shapes that comprise each design are difficult to cut. Part of the original premise for this book (and a premise put to the contributing artists) was to offer patterns that were easy to cut but would represent a major project. There already are a half dozen pattern books for trinkets and no need to add to the list. You will find it far more rewarding to spend a few weeks on a large design that can be installed in a window, than to spend nearly the same amount of time on a lesser project meant to dangle in one.

Some structural and craft information is given in Chapter 3, but it has been kept to a minimum. Techniques, such as painting and etching, that are covered in other books, are not discussed. On the other hand, little has been written on the topic of photographing stained glass, so Chapter 4 has been devoted to that subject.

About the Designs

Each design in Chapter 2 is accompanied by the last name of the contributing artist, the number of pieces in the design, a recommended enlargement size, and other pertinent information so that you will instantly have an idea of what each design represents in terms of work. It is also rather fun to compare the different styles of each artist.

All of the designs are meant to be enlarged, and some methods for enlargement are given in Chapter 1. The suggested sizes tend to be large; if you prefer to work smaller or larger than a specific dimension, adjust the design accordingly. Also, change the designs to suit your tastes and purposes. The more you experiment, the closer you will come to independent designing, but remember to walk before you run.

After interviewing nearly a hundred artists for this book, it was interesting to discover certain similarities. Many people who taught themselves the skills of design and craft wished they had acquired studio discipline right at the beginning. In a studio environment you are given a job to do and expected to show considerable progress after a given period of time. There is no room for feelings of defeat or inadequacy. You simply do the work in front of you and do it well. Working on your own at home, glass can appear to be overwhelmingly difficult. That's just a lot of folderol. It is not so impossible, and you will just have to convince yourself of that truth or lose a lot of time until experience teaches you the same fact.

So, when you begin a project, think professional: plan to complete a design within a prescribed amount of time. When you set down to work, don't get involved with phone calls, friends' visits, or other distractions. Pretend that you are in a studio and that you have eight hours to cut one-hundred pieces or more of glass. When the time is up, you will be amazed with the results.

Go ahead and push for perfect, accurate cutting; demand excellence from yourself with no excuses made in the name of being new at the craft. Always strive for the best.

About the Contributing Artists

The artists whose work is included here are all people that I admire. Regardless of their different levels of ability, directions, and applications, they have met their own personal standards of quality. Since each contributor was approached separately, it is coincidental that The Greenland Studio keeps popping up in the credits. As it happens, this studio does some of the finest work in the country and is a natural draw for talent.

The search for contributors began with mailing open invitations to about fifty craft stores around the United States, placing ads in leading art magazines, and following up every verbal, written, and visual lead that came along. In the end it was an arduous job that took longer than expected. Gradually the list of names was reduced to some forty potential contributors and from those forty came everyone that could meet the original, or second, or third deadline for the book. My only regret for this book is that many talented people could not be represented for one reason or another.

As each design was received (with the exception of five), it had to be enlarged or reduced to 8″ × 10″ (20.3cm × 25.4cm) and redrawn. In the process of doing this my own knowledge of glass design was decidedly improved, enough so that I was tempted to make this a book of eighty-four drawings with a text that said "trace each of these drawings and you will learn a great deal about stained glass design." In fact, "trace each of these drawings and...."

1.

DESIGNING

Principles

The three main principles of good designing are structural strength, responsive color selection, and beautiful design lines. Each factor requires special attention because any single one that is overlooked can ruin the finished project.

Structural strength is often underemphasized. Glass is a nonbiodegradable substance that, barring the possibility of being smashed, can last for hundreds of years. You may not care if your work attains immortality, but wouldn't it be nice if it held together during your lifetime? The trick is to think in terms of use and abuse. Louis Comfort Tiffany's lamps have been tossed into attics and garbage pails and been carted around the world for the last ninety years or so and have still managed to survive. If many of them need restoration work before they can be sold at auction for $20,000 or more, it's forgiveable. The point is, Tiffany has withstood the test of time both artistically and structurally. Regardless of whether or not you like his work, his level of durability is worth aspiring to. Your own work can only be improved in the process.

Nothing can compete with good, clean work that not only looks and feels strong, but that also makes full use of the creative potential of glass. When you want the emphasis to be on color, light, and texture, keep your design lines as simple as possible, but not at the cost of structural strength.

There are a variety of ways to unconsciously undermine your work. For example, be wary of making overly complex designs that are difficult to cut. The limitations of cutting glass are a constant source of irritation, and by pushing these limits, you can "get even" with the medium. However, what you gain in craft expertise you might sacrifice in artistic insight. Only other experienced glass workers and related professionals will recognize what you have accomplished, and they might judge you foolish for your

efforts. The possibility of being ignored or criticized is of no real consequence, but cutting intricate, convoluted shapes that are inherently weak is to be avoided at all costs. The most common shapes to alter are the hourglass, an exaggerated, deep inner curve, and a thin extended tail. The hourglass will crack at the center, the deep inner curve will crack at the apex of its turn, and the extended tail will crack somewhere along the tail or be completely covered with solder. There are other problems that you will encounter but these are the most typical.

If you still long for intricate shapes, then buy an electric diamond band saw and cut spirals in your designs. This tool is expensive, temperamental, and somewhat limited as to the size of the piece it can handle but it will cut a spiral shape (fig. 1-1).

1-1. A letter cut with an electric diamond band saw. Actual size of J is 1" (2.54 cm).

Naturally, these cautionary words refer only to shapes intended for leading and to developing a clearer approach to design. They do not apply to perfecting your cutting abilities. To master the glass cutter, you must constantly practice cutting the most impossible shapes until they become effortless. Just bear in mind that these same shapes take longer to cut, are difficult to lead properly, crack easily, and are not necessarily a proof of your talents.

Color selection is the most time-consuming part of glass working but it is worth every second. The current movement in glass is towards simple lines and textured, clear glass with only a punctuation of color. This is possibly a reaction to all that is overstated and overstimulating in Western culture. Art movements, however, are only indications and at best, clairvoyant indications of the future. They are not rules. Your inner world takes priority over any movement and if you are filled with abundant color and curling lines, who cares if it's passé—do it! Keep in mind that more is less, and that although you want to be concise, be yourself if it kills you.

As you work, think of the thrust of the work in terms of color and clout. Glass has a very powerful effect on the subconscious. This may be due in part to light passing through the medium and changing the environment and everything else it touches. The intense jewel-like colors in old church windows create a perfect setting conducive to somber yet enlightened meditation. Traditional church music has a similar effect and when the two are combined, it is positively hypnotic. Color and light in stained glass are very closely related to music on other levels, most specifically in the sounds and silences found in music. The architect, Le Corbusier, built rhythms into his buildings by using clear light windows and open areas that create a kind of musical morse code, da-dit-da-da and so on. It is impossible to walk through one of his structures without feeling the staccato beat of his imagination. So, when you are working on a project, especially one intended for natural lighting, envision the full scope of what you want to convey. Vary the areas of color and their relative proportions. If something feels wrong, trust your intuition and try other colors. If it becomes too confusing, step back, let your eyes take a rest, or ask other people what they think of different combinations. Second opinions, especially when ignored, help to solidify and clarify your own intentions.

Many types of glass show dramatic changes within the same sheet of glass, either in swirling clouds of two or more colors or in texture and transparency. Seek out the nuances of these changes. Trap a large bubble between the lead lines, or use the color change from light to dark to show depth in a flower petal or spread the swirling areas of color throughout a design so they appear and disappear in judicious spots. As an exercise, cut the same design a few different times with entirely new glass selections (see fig. C-4).

If you ever get the opportunity to see a quantity of colored glass, such as can be found on the five floors of S.A. Bendheim Company, Inc. in New York City, you might just go wild with joy, then suddenly feel utter dismay. There is so much from which to choose that it is almost impossible to find a starting point. Not since the days of LaFarge and Tiffany has there been such an abundance of glass. In fact, the full range is awesome. Without years of practical experience (and even then, the following still applies) always make a colored drawing of your design before choosing glass. It might seem like a bothersome, unnecessary step to work out a colored rendition of your project, but it isn't. You can always change your mind but it is invaluable to have some sort of predetermined guide as a reference.

Regardless of the material that you use to make an 8″ × 10″ (20.3cm by 25.4cm) colored drawing, be it watercolor, colored pencils, colored paper, or felt-tip pens, the colors will never exactly match those of glass. They will be flat and lifeless in comparison. Furthermore, stained glass has very definite visual weights that are different from anything you could imitate with pen or pencil. However, without the colored drawing, you would be choosing colors blindly.

When you are selecting glass, always make sure that you hold the glass up to the light source for which it is intended. Glass colors change dramatically depending upon the light source and it is easy to be misled. A sheet of blue glass, seen under fluorescent light in a store can turn out to be turquoise when seen in a window lighted by daylight. It will appear to be yet another color under incandescent light. This attention to color control must be maintained once you begin actual work. If you are working on a design that is meant to be artificially lighted, then place that type of light (incandescent, or fluorescent) beneath your light box. If it is to be lighted naturally, it is best to work on an easel, against daylight.

A light box is almost self-descriptive. It is a box with ventilation that has a plate-glass top and receptacles for lights beneath the glass. An easel, in essence, is a sheet of plate glass on which the lead lines of a design have been painted, that is then mounted in a window. By laying the plate glass over the design, you can paint on the lead lines with poster paint. When this is done, the plate glass is secured in a window and the newly cut pieces of glass are stuck into position with small gobs of Plasticine or Mortite caulking putty available in hardware stores. If a color is wrong, the piece is easily removed and a new piece cut and stuck in its place. Later, all of the pieces are removed, cleaned, and leaded together. The plate glass can be cleaned with a razor and the putty discarded.

Glass is always a dangerous medium. With this fact in mind, you can put together your own flexible structures, but always keep children, friends, pets, and bad tempers at a safe distance.

The third principle, beautiful design lines, is the theme of this book.

What is it that makes something beautiful? Is it really only in the eyes of the beholder, or is there some universal truth that transcends everything else? These questions have been bantered around for ages past and will continue to fire up personalities for ages to come, with or without my comments. The ability to create beauty is not something that can be infused into your personality. You either have it, or you have it and don't know how to tap your resources. This may be why so many people think themselves totally lacking in creativity and yet go on to be masterful cooks, decorate their homes with flair and imagination, or wear clothes with a special pizzaz. Speaking can be another creative outlet and yet the same people who swear by their lack of artistic talent can hold their friends spellbound with a story of some trivial experience. Cooking, nonprofessional decorating, selecting clothes, and storytelling are a few examples of the many things that we do creatively and yet do not call art, but they are expressions of art. The same effort and intelligence that goes into decorating a home can be channeled into other creative areas. Think about this; all of these directions have one thing in common, they all deal with visible, tangible objects or experienced events. The nearest equivalent in art would be in the areas of three-dimensional materials—clay, wood, and even metal. The problem is that once you leave the three-dimensional world and lay pen to paper on a one-dimensional plane, you enter the world of abstract thought.

Abstract thought comes naturally to a very few people or there would be more than one Leonardo da Vinci to an age. For the rest of us, abstraction is a learned ability. Do you remember, or maybe still have, some of your earliest drawings from childhood? If not, look at some children's drawings. They might make you recall your own beginnings. Children lop off the top of their peoples' heads, place the figure at the bottom of the page, turn their figures at side views or front views only, and are wildly inaccurate as to relative sizes (The little dog that stands next to the person is truly a miniature.) As children progress through the school system, someone (teacher, parent, or peer) tells them to round

off the top of the head, place the figure in the center of the page, add a horizon line, and to make the little dog a bit bigger. The figures improve but they are often still drawn in side or full frontal position.

To draw a person in partial profile is to understand how a three-dimensional object distorts on a flat surface so that it still appears to be three dimension...a bit tricky to say the least. A common mistake is the size of the hand in relation to the size of the face. The hand is actually as large as the face and once this is pointed out, it seems so obvious that you wonder why it was never apparent before. To those people that refute their creative abilities and "cannot draw a straight line," the correct proportioning of the human figure on paper must seem like magic. It isn't and never was. Anyone who so desires can be shown how to draw an accurate rendition of the human figure or any other object. It only takes one person to lean over your shoulder and casually point out the obvious to forever destroy the illusion of art as magic.

The issue here then is work and development as opposed to the mystical manufacture of creativity. It is safe to assume that you are already seeking ways to fully realize your own sense of beauty and design or you would not have purchased a book on design. Although you may want to change the percentages somewhat, art is ten-percent raw creative energy and ninety-percent work, acquired knowledge, and sweat. Or as the oh-so-specific Thomas Edison is credited with saying, "Genius is one percent inspiration and ninety-nine percent perspiration."

The expression "I don't know anything about art, but I know what I like" is an excellent starting point, in spite of the negative connotations it may have accumulated over the years. If you can locate and pinpoint your inclinations, it then becomes a matter of repeated practice to develop these leanings. This is not a recommendation to copy another artist's style but simply to study and learn from what has gone before. When you see a work of art that pleases you, stop and figure out exactly what it is that you find so enjoyable. It is more helpful to analyze what it is that you like about something than to mull over your dislikes. Always work from a position of strength.

Getting a clear perspective and maintaining your creative attention are problems for all artists, regardless of their medium; visual arts, dance, music, writing, etc. It seems that after working on a project for a long time, the ability to judge your own work is lost. Possibly it's a matter of overexposure. Try smelling six perfumes in a row and you'll get the idea. There are many ways to restimulate your senses, the best of which is to take yourself off to a lovely island for a long weekend and forget the whole business for a few days. You might also try taping the design on which you are working to a wall and just looking at it as you go about your everyday life. Whenever you notice a line to be removed or added, take the drawing down, make the changes, and tape it back to the wall. You may see improvements on Thursday that were not obvious on Monday. The very idea of "getting a new perspective" is self explanatory...go and get one: tape the drawing upside down, hold it in a mirror, or toss it on the floor and stand on a chair to look at it. Although this all sounds rather silly and is, it works. Besides, when you're desperate, you'll try anything.

Another important aspect of designing for stained glass is your artistic direction and style. Basically all design is either a form of realism or abstraction. Both general categories have many off-shoots and both have their own particular merits. Even if you consider a certain style to be an abomination, the style should be mastered anyway, if only for the discipline. It is always harder to work on something alien to your natural inclinations but a great deal can be learned from the exercise. It is only through total exposure that you really learn and define your own sense of beauty.

Another reason for mastering different styles is to prepare you to sell your work. Commissions are wonderful occurances. They not only help to support the art habit, but also force you to work when you would rather be lazy and give you impetus to complete works of art. All these benefits, plus the pride of selling your work, will be denied if you are too rigid to bend with the wishes of the client. This is not to say that you should become a pawn to the almighty dollar or dracma, simply that after you complete a work of art, someone else must live with it on a day-to-day basis. If the work reflects only your ideas and does not take into account the tastes and spirit of the person by whom you have been commissioned, then the art is ultimately inadequate. Therefore, in order to develop a flexible and knowledgeable response to design, all styles should be considered equally.

Design Sources

Finding sources for inspiration can be as simple as walking down the street, looking through a book, or taking slides of things that please you. An imaginative mind can make use of reflections in water, the lines in Cubist paintings, machinery, or architecture and find inspiration in pieces of broken glass, a cloud formation, or listening to music. Sources for ideas abound in everything that touches the senses.

The human creature has a well-developed knack for borrowing great ideas from unlikely sources. The scrunch-faced little night bat is directly responsible for sonar, which affected world history, and the chambered nautilus seashell has aided the twin causes of romance and intrigue for centuries through the gift of the spiral staircase. No matter how terrific the original source of information, it is still only beauty in the raw without human interpretation and adaptation. To really make use of what already exists, without abusing it, is an art in itself. How many millions of minds examined a chambered nautilus before one struck upon the idea of a staircase along a similar plan?

When designing for stained glass, the same processes of interpretation and adaptation must be brought into play. The eye can be conditioned to translate thoughts and impressions of existing reality (or fantasy) into the medium of glass. To this end and as a way of immediately learning something about design, you can try this experiment. Next time you flip through a magazine, pick out a photograph, advertisement, or illustration that looks suitable for stained glass and draw in some lead lines. In many cases the final outcome will be a mass of black lines that overpower the original idea but often the result will be a very workable design. Always use the fewest lines possible to describe the image, and if you really like the design, make a tracing of it and cut it in glass.

Art is a habit of the mind that should be encouraged at every opportunity. Get used to ripping out pictures from magazines, taking snapshots of interesting shapes and images, and jotting down ideas that pop up. Many artists accumulate this type of personal reference file since good ideas are too easily forgotten.

The more you work with glass the more you will discover your own style until it is as recognizable as a signature. Individual style encompasses everything from the type of cuts you prefer to make, their complexity and basic shape, to favorite ways of combining line, color, and texture. The speed with which you make these discoveries is important. Because glass is so time consuming, anything that can save you extra, unnecessary work is very desirable. It is equally important to understand the difference between trying to save time and trying to take shortcuts that undercut your efforts.

Realism or representational design is, and always has been, very popular. The best way to work is directly from nature. If you are sketching out a floral design, then purchase that type of flower and draw it until you have the flower in a few different positions. You may encounter a few problems, however, when it's the middle of winter and you want to design an array of dogwood blossoms in full bloom. Alas, even if it is summer and the hills, full of dogwood trees, you may not have the slightest idea of how to draw them nor the time to teach yourself. Besides researching the flower in design books at your library, there is another solution. Enter the camera, stage left, and with all the fanfare worthy of a star.

The camera has become one of the main tools for at least one form of art, Photo-Realism (also known as Trompe l'Oeil and by other names). This style depends almost entirely upon the camera for the initial image. The Photo-Realist painting of *Les Deux Vasches* by Venturella (see fig. 1-2) was started in exactly this manner. (The original painting is oil on linen and measures 44″ × 66″ (1.1m × 1.68m). The camera is just a tool for laying out the beginning image. It is not cheating to make use of this tool because it only does one-quarter of the work and the other three-quarters must come from you. Imagine for a moment that you want to do a cityscape in glass; so, you sit down in front of a window that looks out on a city and start to sketch. If you have the training, you may have the drawing worked out in a matter of hours. The camera approach is to take slide photographs of the same view from a few different angles and possibly with a few different lenses and then study the results. In this way you will have a group of shots showing all of the buildings in correct proportion to each other plus any dramatic lighting effect present at the time of the shooting. Also, since the image on the slide must be projected on a slide projector and the slide projector can be used to enlarge the image to almost any size, you can automatically choose which part of the scene to cut in glass and how large you want the finished design to be.

With the sketching method, unless you work "to size," the drawing will have to be enlarged before it can be cut in glass, the buildings may not be in correct proportion to each other, interesting lighting effects may be lost, and all you wanted in the first place was an accurate rendition of what you saw. Using the camera to solve certain problems is another example of making the work as easy as possible. The shortest distance between two points is a straight line and as long as you are not sacrificing anything in the process, then take the most efficient route.

Another use for the camera is in working with the alphabet. Pick up a typeface sample book from an art store and you will have fifty different styles of lettering, many of which can be adapted for glass. Photograph the alphabet that you want to use on slide film and project it onto the wall to the size you desire. Then by moving a piece of paper around the wall, you can pick up the letters that you need. The finished work or words can then be painted onto glass or adapted for cutting in glass. If you prefer to work more freely, the typeface book can be used for reference as you make up your own lettering style (see fig. 1–3).

1-2

1-3.   A simple method for adapting Gothic letters to be cut in glass and a typical background. Free-style company logo by Stacy Baum and Chester Gelband.

The camera can also be used to photograph drawings or other photographs from books or a few different slides can be sandwiched together to make a composite image. The possibilities are endless. Keep in mind that all designs that are worked out with this method will still have to be altered somewhat in order to be cut in glass. The camera is ignorant of the limitations of glass.

Representing the human figure has its own unique problems. Unlike animals, flowers, machines, and cracks in the sidewalk, we happen to be human and care deeply how we are depicted. The area of particular sensitivity centers around the face. Picasso-like abstractions are more acceptable than attempts at realism that fail, if only because the world has had a few years to become accustomed to his style. In fact, the painting *Guernica*, is so closely related to stained glass design that it is interesting that Picasso never had it cut in glass.

If you want to cut the face in glass, plan on using an exaggerated facial expression (see fig. 1–4) and/or a prop of some sort. Always avoid the simple puppet line that connects the nose to the mouth because it gives the face a dour expression. Instead, add more wrinkles, wisps of hair, a hand

strategically placed, or an object that breaks up the features in an acceptable way (see Chapter 2, design 47). In lieu of cutting the figure in glass, experiment with acid etching, cold painting, paint that requires firing, or a photographic technique (see Chapter 3).

The photographs and accompanying illustrations show how some designs originated and how they were translated into glass. The translations are rather simplistic and straight forward in nature, involving slight adjustments to meet the demands of the medium and/or isolating the figure from the background. This approach to glass design cer-

1-5

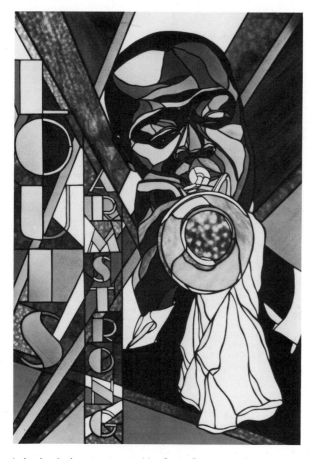

1-4. Louis Armstrong panel by Stacy Baum and Chester Gelband for the Cotton Club in New York City.

1-6

18

tainly has its limits but it at least frees you from the need for pattern books such as this one. (It is important to note that if you adapt a famous character like Spiderman and then mass produce the design without prior agreement with Marvel Comics, you can be sued for plagiarism.)

Abstract design is a wonderfully obtuse topic. Inspiration can come from any direction; music, some tactile sensation, a slanted ray of light, or even language. The problem lies in how to interpret these stimuli in a way that even vaguely represents your feelings. The solution, which somehow falls short of believability, is to study, disect, debate, examine, and generally devour all that is abstract. This could include obscure foreign films, oil slick patterns, and schools of philosophy that you normally wouldn't approach on a bet. In order to view things in an abstract perspective, you must become a bit abstracted yourself without, of course, losing a grip on reality.

One fairly painless and instructive introduction to abstract thought is to work with geometric design. Geometry forces your attention on structure, visual balance, and the importance of color. By eliminating the distraction of curving lines and representational interpretation, your concentration shifts from the decorative qualities of line work to the more utilitarian function of leading. Once you understand how to distribute the physical and visual weights of glass, the jump to the freer forms of abstract design is slightly shortened. The most exciting aspect of abstract design is that you sometimes come within a hair of describing the indescribable. A fellow by the name of Arthur Waite defined it perfectly in his book, *The Pictorial Key to the Tarot*, when he ended his explanation on the Two of Cups as being "that desire which is not in Nature, but by which Nature is sanctified." It is difficult, yet not impossible, to turn the whimsical meanderings of the mind into tangible works of art. When it happens, and it seems to happen most frequently with abstract design, the sense of elation is (naturally) indescribable.

1-7

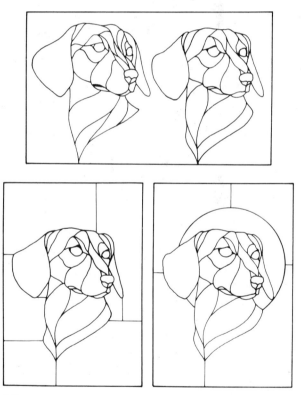

1-8

1-9. *Stingray* (1955), bronze sculpture by Alma Kline. (Photo by Jeremiah W. Russell)

1-11

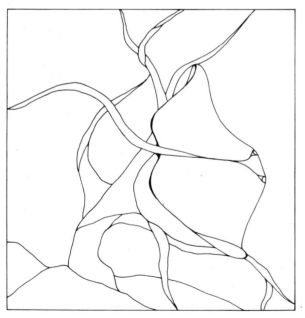

1-10

1-12

One of the many freedoms of working with abstract design is that lines can be added or removed on whim, as long as structural strength has been accounted for. With representational and geometric design, many lines are necessary simply because they complete the pattern or picture. Pure abstract design also encourages daring color selection and the maximum use of the variations within a sheet of glass.

Glass is a most versatile and exciting material. It can be spun into fabric, made into coiled springs, cut with a saw, drilled, etched, painted, blown, pulled like taffy, shaped with heat, and even made unbreakable. Do not rush the experience, but instead, savor it slowly and thoroughly.

Enlarging Designs

The best way to design for stained glass is to work to exact size. If your finished piece is to measure 5′ × 3′ (1.5m × .9m), then work on a sheet of paper slightly larger than those dimensions taped to the wall. (A small color sketch can be made later to aid in glass selection). If, however, you are not inclined to work to size, or if you wish to use designs from this book or others, you will have to know how to enlarge a pattern. The general methods of enlarging include: camera and slide projector, opaque projector, photocopy, graph paper and grids, and Pantograph. Each method has advantages and disadvantages.

Camera and Slide Projector

This method is excellent, although if you do not already own a 35mm camera and a projector, the initial cost is steep. The only justification for this kind of investment is that you will use the equipment for shooting your work as well as for making design enlargements. The procedure is simple. Lay the design that you want to enlarge on a flat table, shine some light on it, and take a slide photograph from directly above the design (see fig. 1-13A and B). After the slide is processed, tape a large sheet of paper to a wall and draw in the outside dimensions of the proposed work. Shut off the room lights, project the slide onto the paper until it fills the outline, and draw over the projected image. If the photograph was taken from a slight angle there will be some distortion so always check the parallel lines and right angles of the projected design with a large right triangle and a ruler. Some distortion can be corrected by tilting the projector.

1-13. Make sure that the camera is parallel and at right angles to the subject that you want to reproduce; otherwise distortion will occur.

Opaque Projector

The opaque projector is accurate, fast, and simple to use but the best models cost as much as a camera. Also, even the top-of-the-line models require a fairly dark room for accurate projection. To use an opaque projector, turn off the room lights, place the design to be enlarged in or on the machine, and aim the projected image onto a large sheet of paper taped to the wall. As with the camera and slide projector method, it is best to draw in the desired outline beforehand and to check all straight lines and right angles with a plastic triangle and ruler. If you are buying equipment and must choose between an opaque projector and a camera and slide projector, the latter is the better choice. Once you learn to work to size, the opaque projector is rarely needed, whereas the photographic equipment will continue to be useful.

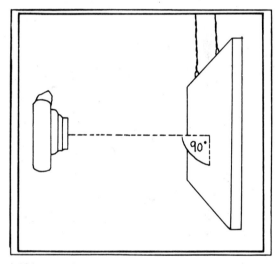

1-13A

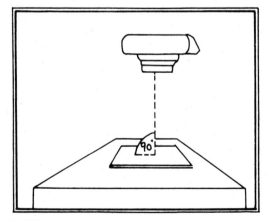

1-13B

Photocopy

Having enlargements made commercially on a photocopy machine appears to be relatively inexpensive and fast. However, over a period of time it can become costly if you enlarge many designs. The degree of enlargement possible is also limited to certain sizes. If your finished piece is to be quite large, you may have to enlarge it in sections and then tape the sections together for a working pattern. Check the *Yellow Pages* of your telephone directory to see what photocopy services are available in your area and then contact a few companies to find out what is possible and to compare costs.

Graph Paper and Grids

This is a tried and true, inexpensive method of enlargement, although it is tedious and time consuming. First the original design is divided into small squares and then a larger sheet of paper, with the desired outline drawn in, is divided into the same number of squares. The lines from the small grid are located on the larger grid, and gradually the pattern is formed.

Pantograph

The Pantograph is an extension arm that has a pencil on one end and a metal tip on the other. Once the enlargement scale is set on the Pantograph, you trace around the original design with the metal tip and the penciled end makes an enlarged copy. It is an inexpensive and inaccurate tool with limited ability to enlarge.

Reworking Designs

The reason that you rework a design is to save time in the long run. The object is to maintain the essence of the design while refining the lines. It may take ten pages of tracing paper and a few days' work to reach the goal of a single good pattern. Changes can be full of subtle nuance that have little effect on the original or be so drastic as to make the original and final drawing unrelated. Reworking the design begins with the first few sketches and can proceed right up through the last soldering stage. Be prepared to change your mind throughout the work in case it proves necessary. The more work you put into the primary drawing stage the smaller the chance of having to make major changes later on.

The following illustrations show some ways of reworking designs. The original drawing (fig. 1-14) of the motorcyclist was taken from a photograph in a racing magazine. In spite of its realistic source, the design looks rigid and cartoonish. Tracing paper was used to save only the most necessary lines and the drawing was reworked from those lines (fig. 1-

15). Other than just simplifying and reducing the number of lines, the only major change was to give the racer a new, easier-to-cut helmet. By doing away with unnecessary lines, the figure is more believably in motion.

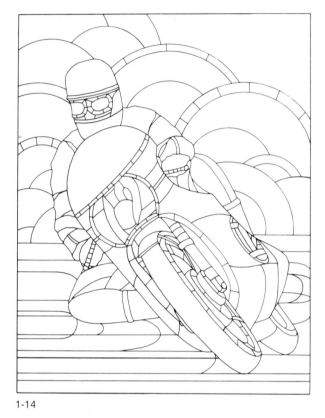

1-14

1-15

In the second set of drawings, the original free-hand sketch (fig. 1-16) seemed to fall off the edge of the paper in a lop-sided manner. By holding a mirror up to the design, (fig. 1-17) it was possible to see an interesting way of balancing the design (fig. 1-18). Tracing paper was then used to work out the repeat image and to eliminate some of the center lines which were distracting in their abundance.

The third example shows how you might totally deviate from the original idea. For three weeks the drawing (fig. 1-19) was left taped to the workroom wall. The design was basically dull and uninspiring; however, when it was finally taken down and re-worked, it metamorphosed into something new altogether (fig. 1-20). Some of the original lines are still present but they can only be seen when the two drawings are laid over each other.

It is not always immediately apparent as to how a design will work out. More often than not, you will have only a vague feeling about possible improvements but nothing in detail. Besides, once you make one change it has an effect on the rest of the drawing and additional changes may become necessary. As you rework a drawing, make sure that every curve, dip, and angle are to your liking. Investigate every possibility for answers and challenge your solutions until thoroughly convinced that the design is not only pleasing but also structurally sound and that all of the individual pieces that make up the whole are within your cutting abilities.

Buy inexpensive tracing paper by the roll, and rather than using an eraser to make changes, sketch in the changes on the tracing paper. In this way you have a record of your progress that allows you to abandon one direction and pick up on another without losing any important, hastily erased lines. Often, just by the act of redrawing the same design a few times, an intangible understanding takes over and everything miraculously falls into place.

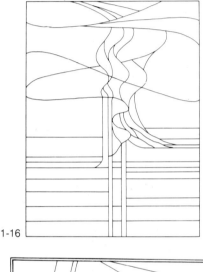
1-16

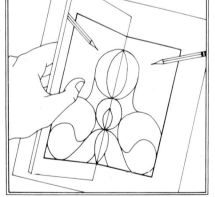
1-17

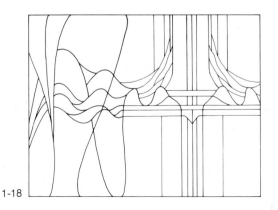
1-18

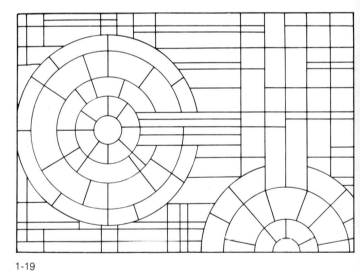
1-19

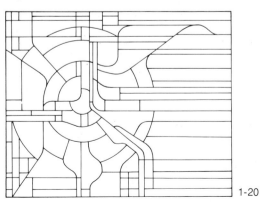
1-20

1-21

Cropping

One simple method for reworking a design is to crop or reframe the perimeters of the design. Figures 1-21 through 1-24 show how a single design can be changed depending upon how it is cropped. In some instances the design had to be extended to fit within the new framing and in one instance another use of the mirror image technique was brought into play.

To make a simple cropping tool that will help you to visualize how a drawing can be changed, cut two L shapes out of cardboard and place them over a drawing (see fig. 1-25).

1-23

1-22

1-24

1-25

Another type of selective cropping involves enlarging the design and using a small part of the original. This technique is useful when you have to cope with too many small pieces or when you want to make a design more dramatic by making the eye focus its attention on just the main figure and eliminating most of the background. The original drawing (fig. 1-26) is fine as is if you have lots of time and a love for small work. The first enlargement (fig. 1-27) and cropping is better than the original because it reduces the difficulties and amount of craft work without destroying the basic idea. The second enlargement and cropping (fig. 1-28) further simplifies the design but has the emotional effect of King Kong peeking into your window. Notice what part of the original design was used to make the two enlargements (fig. 1-29).

1-26

1-28

1-27

1-29

26

Relative Proportions

Whenever you work with designs that have definite backgrounds and foregrounds, whether they be abstract or realistic in nature, the relative proportions can be altered. In the original drawing (fig. 1-30) the fly is alright but the background is overly busy. By enlarging the background while keeping the fly a constant size (fig. 1-31), the design is instantly easier to read and much of the craft work is done away with. The second enlargement (fig. 1-32) is the best choice since the background is now quite large and simple to craft plus the design still retains its original feeling. The centers of the geometric shapes were changed to avoid large lumps of solder or lead from meeting at those points. In both enlargements, slight changes were made to the fly—moving a wing, increasing the body size, moving a leg etc.—so that the fly would fit in with the new background.

There are many other ways to rework a design and if you keep that concept in mind, your work will inevitably reflect the effort.

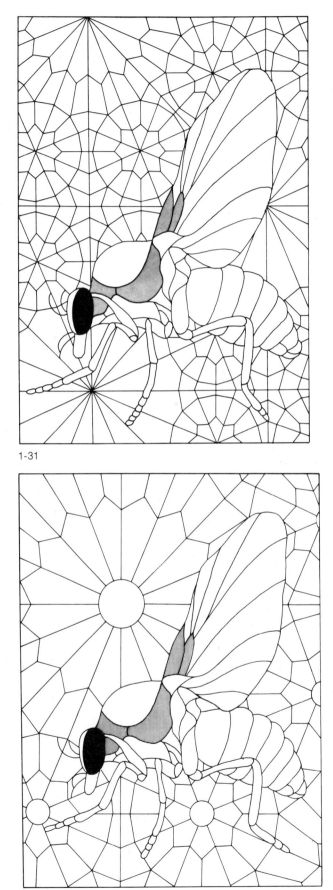

1-31

1-30

1-32

27

Cold Turkey

One aspect of designing that is difficult to understand through drawings, photographs, or study is the cold approach, which is to say, working up a design without any obvious source of inspiration except that which comes from the depths of your own imagination. The question is, how do you do it? How do you simply sit down and create art? The answer is, you don't. The creative urge rarely appears on demand. It is a will-of-the-wisp thing that comes and goes without warning. If you plan to work only when you are inspired, then you must also plan to stay near your studio area and do a lot of waiting. Instead of waiting for the perfect moment to begin, do a lot of designing, experimenting, and glasswork and expect about ten percent of it to be truly inspired. You should also expect the other ninety percent to be nothing less than your best effort. There is nothing more aggravating than really wanting to do something and not having the wherewithal to do it. The idea of "doing your homework" is as true as it is obnoxious. You must strive to make the craft end of glasswork and designing as effortless as possible so that the special inspired moments will not be wasted.

As you develop technical abilities, learn how to recognize the energy surge that is part of creativity. It will happen that on certain days, for no apparent reason, everything goes smoothly; you have the Midas touch. More likely than not, you are experiencing a creative, energy surge. The same surge, if you are physically oriented, would make you want to run around or if you are a sociable person, to call a friend. For the visually oriented, it is a perfect time to draw. There are other times that are also peak creative moments and they may occur when you feel drained, numb, or depressed, but if you can first learn to recognize the most obvious times, then the other moments will become more apparent.

Besides perfecting the mechanics of glass and your own personal mechanics, finding a good place to work is also very important. Some famous artists do all of their preliminary sketching on the backs of napkins in the middle of busy restaurants and some writers do all of their writing in bed with the phone unplugged. Find out where and what helps you to create. What is your best setting: silence and solitude or Grand Central Station? Work on the floor or in bed, turn on the radio, television, record player, or turn them off, until you learn your most comfortable spots. Then you will be ready with the skills, the awareness, and the right place to work for the next time you feel elated. When that time comes along, don't misunderstand the feeling and call a friend to chat. Set yourself down and draw (fig. 1-33).

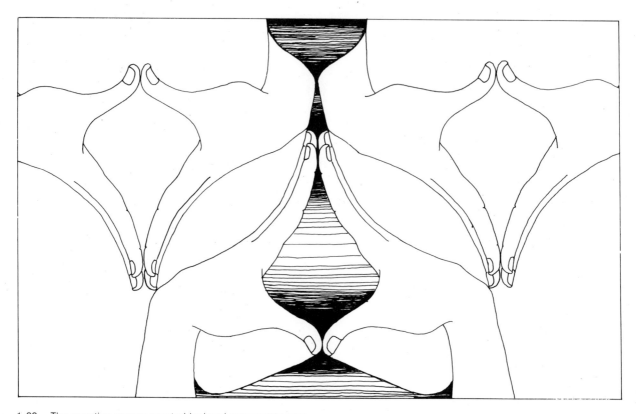

1-33. The negative spaces created by hand movements may have inspired ancient Middle Eastern design.

2.

DESIGNS

Following are 84 designs for study and practice. For each design the last name of the artist, the number of pieces in the pattern, the recommended enlargement size (to the nearest full inch), and other related information is provided to give you an idea of the work involved and to allow you to compare individual styles. All of these designs must be enlarged (see Chapter 1). Since the suggested measurements given tend to be large, you may want to work smaller. It is generally easier to cut large designs, but the larger you work, the more serious is the need for reinforcement.

If you are working in lead came, all lines are sight size and you will have to allow room for the heart of the lead. Also, with lead came, circles and ovals are meant to "kiss" (see Chapter 3).

The patterns are divided into three major categories: abstract, representational, and three-dimensional. Some designs will invariably be easier to cut than others, but they are all within the capabilities of first-year work. If one seems overly difficult, then add extra lead lines to make it easier. Even if you are in midwork, designs can be altered.

Abstract

1. Garber, 92 pieces, 24″ (60.96cm) in diameter.
2. Bakst, 42 pieces, 17″ × 23″ (43.18cm × 58.42cm). Circles are meant to "kiss."
3. French, 71 pieces, 20″ × 30″ (50.8cm × 76.2cm). Taken from a photograph of cracks in the sidewalk.
4. Revere, 221 pieces, 26″ (66.04cm) in diameter.
5. Greenbaum, 47 pieces, 11″ × 32″ (27.94cm × 81.28 cm). Best worked in antique glass. See fig. C-4.
6. Hyams, 105 pieces, 44″ × 26″ (111.76cm × 66.04cm). Eight points must be resolved within the design.
7. Furman, 189 pieces, 22″ × 34″ (55.88cm × 86.36cm).
8. Bakst, 83 pieces, 19″ × 35″ (48.26cm × 88.9cm).
9. Myers, 322 pieces, each panel is 12″ × 24″ (30.48cm × 60.96cm). The thick black areas indicate where to float solder or use a metal overlay technique.
10. Wilkinson/Feller, 81 pieces, 24″ × 28″ (60.96cm × 71.12cm).
11. French, 45 pieces (not counting circles), 20″ × 32″ (50.8cm × 81.28cm). Circles can be cut from glass or substituted with rondelles. Black areas indicate where to float solder. From the Grossberg residence, New York, New York.
12. Cushen, (A) 120 pieces, enlarge to standard window frame size; (B) 53 pieces, enlarge to standard window frame size. Both from the Ward residence, Forest Hills, New York.
13. French, (A) 180 pieces, 26″ (66.04cm) along base; (B) 74 pieces, 26″ (66.04cm) along base. Notice how these patterns differ in their number of pieces and yet seem equally busy.
14. Revere, 409 pieces, 20″ (50.8cm) square. First cut the glass into long strips and then cut off the individual pieces rather than cutting each piece of glass separately.
15. Bakst, 39 pieces, 20″ (50.8cm) square.
16. Hyams, 168 pieces, 23″ × 28″ (58.42cm × 17.12cm). This design was originally made much larger.

As an indication of this, the wide black lines were meant to be 2″ wide (5.08cm) lead came. From the Adar residence, Scarsdale, New York.

17. French, 169 pieces, 16″ (40.64cm) along the diagonal. Adapted from a Chinese lattice design.

18. Venturella, 126 pieces, 32″ × 35″ (81.28cm × 88.9cm). At these measurements, the design is for three separate windows but if made larger, then the two central divisions would be reinforcing bars.

19. Avidon (1973), 238 pieces, 36″ × 42″ (91.44cm × 106.58cm). Cut glass into long strips and then remove the individual pieces.

20. Furman, *Harley Davidson Sunset*, 190 pieces, 12′ × 47″ (30.48cm × 119.38cm).

21. Garber, 36 pieces, 20″ × 31″ (50.8 × 78.74cm). If lower circle is too difficult to cut as is, divide the area by adding a line.

22. French, 99 pieces, 15″ × 22″ (38.1cm × 55.88cm).

23. Greenbaum, *Flight*, 49 pieces, 19″ × 29″ (48.26cm × 73.66cm).

24. Bakst, 88 pieces, 20″ (50.8cm) square.

25. Hyams, 121 pieces, 17″ × 45″ (43.18cm × 114.3cm). Originally designed to be much larger. There are at least nine difficult cuts within the design. From the Klein residence, Oradell, New Jersey.

26. Wilkinson, 284 pieces, 36″ (91.44cm) in diameter. See fig. C-17.

27. French, 77 pieces, 34″ × 26″ (86.36cm × 66.04cm).

28. Hyams, 91 pieces, large panel 20″ × 21″ (50.8cm × 53.34cm); small panel 20″ × 9″ (50.8cm × 22.86cm). Originally meant to be much larger. From the Grammatica residence, Forest Hills, New York.

29. French, 115 pieces, 20″ × 16″ (50.8cm × 40.64cm). See fig. C-10.

30. Greenbaum, 42 pieces, 25″ × 43″ (63.5cm × 109.22cm).

31. Wilkinson, 96 pieces, 21″ × 31″ (53.34cm × 78.74cm). Cut glass into long strips and then remove the individual pieces.

32. Bakst, 45 pieces, 17″ × 23″ (43.18cm × 58.42cm).

33. Scarborough, 75 pieces, 20″ (50.8cm) square.

34. Avidon (1977), 101 pieces, 30″ × 60″ (76.2cm × 152.4cm).

35. LBJ, 95 pieces, 26″ × 19″ (66.04cm × 48.26cm). French adaptation of a drawing by Larry Brooks.

Representational

36. French, 306 pieces, 28″ × 46″ (71.12cm × 116.84cm). These dimensions will make the zebra stripes easy to cut but the area over the rump may need another line to make the large piece of glass more manageable. If the pattern is made smaller, paint or etch in the stripes and cut the outline as drawn.

37. Sell, 126 pieces, 34″ × 43″ (86.36cm × 109.22cm).

38. Cullenbine, *White Tiger*, 54 pieces, 23″ × 19″ (58.42cm × 48.26cm). The area between the lower jaw and extended paw will be easier to cut if divided by more lines. Shading indicates light and dark areas within a sheet of glass.

39. French, 224 pieces, 19″ × 25″ (48.26cm × 63.5cm).

40. Nugget, 22 pieces, 25″ × 6″ (63.5cm × 15.24cm). Float solder in dark areas.

41. French, 238 pieces, 27″ × 29″ (68.58cm × 73.66cm).

42. Furman, 130 pieces, 35″ × 16″ (88.9cm × 40.64cm).

43. Nugget, 131 pieces, approximately 23″ × 15″ (58.42cm × 38.1cm). Float solder in the dark areas. To cut the design smaller, use glass nuggets in the centers of the flowers instead of cutting them from glass.

44. French, *Great Horned Owl*, 379 pieces, 32″ × 37″ (81.28cm × 93.98cm).

45. Myers, 47 pieces, 14″ × 23″ (35.56cm × 58.42cm).

46. Cullenbine, *Mule Deers*, 192 pieces, 35″ × 44″ (88.9cm × 111.76cm). The area over the rump will be easier to cut if divided by another line. Also, the area around the stag's ear can be simplified.

47. DeBerardinis, 223 pieces, 29″ × 26″ (73.66cm × 66.04cm). Note how the fans interrupt the features and make it possible to cut the faces.

48. French, 321 pieces, 24″ × 27″ (60.96cm × 68.58cm). To cut the pattern smaller, simplify the feathers.

49. Myers, 176 pieces, 18″ × 27″ (45.72cm × 68.58cm). Vary the width of the leaded or foiled line by metal overlay or floating solder.

50. Mellen, *Crab Grass*, 189 pieces, 24″ × 28″ (60.96cm × 71.12cm).

51. French, 128 pieces, 20″ × 26″ (50.80cm × 66.04cm).

52. Kline, 41 pieces, 17″ × 17″ (43.18cm × 42.55cm).

53. Nugget, 39 pieces, approximately 16″ (40.64cm) in diameter. This free-form design can be turned into a mirror. If you expect difficulty in cutting the mirror to fit around the flowers, add another flower or leaf to fill the spaces.

54. French, adaptation of Spiderman (Copyright © 1977 by Marvel Comics Group. All rights reserved), 405 pieces, 31″ × 47″ (78.74cm × 119.38cm). Cut all of the web patterns in large sections and then divide up the sections rather than cutting each piece separately.

55. Garber, 167 pieces, 13″ × 32″ (33.02cm × 81.28cm).

56. Myers, 41 pieces, 26″ × 17″ (66.04cm × 43.18cm). Use metal overlay or paint on the beaks and feet. Shading indicates light and dark areas within the glass.

57. French, 130 pieces, 30″ × 23″ (76.2cm × 58.42cm). Design can be cut smaller by simplifying the eye area. Float solder or use metal overlay on the dark areas.

58. Baum, *Sunflower Triptych*, 24″ × 34″ (60.96cm × 86.36cm).

59. Cardea, 100 pieces, 28″ × 13″ (71.12cm × 33.02cm).

60. French, 354 pieces, 24″ × 29″ (60.96cm × 73.66cm).

61. Kiaulénas, 86 pieces, 27″ × 23″ (68.58cm × 58.42cm).

62. Garber, 234 pieces, 31″ × 13″ (78.74cm × 33.02cm).

63. French, 56 pieces, 17″ × 22″ (43.18cm × 55.88cm).

64. Cullenbine, *Hawk*, 160 pieces, 37″ × 44″ (93.98cm × 111.76cm).

65. French, 90 pieces, 18″ × 19″ (45.72cm × 48.26cm).

66. Mellen, *Fighting Dragons*, 715 pieces, 28″ × 44″ (71.12cm × 111.76cm). See fig. C-27.

67. Baum, 167 pieces, 22″ × 35″ (55.88cm × 88.90cm).

68. French, 131 pieces, 24″ × 31″ (60.96cm × 78.74cm).

69. Cullenbine, *Mongoose & Mamba*, 108 pieces, 21″ × 33″ (53.34cm × 83.82cm). Either paint, drill, and/or etch the eye areas.

70. French, *Minnesota*, 244 pieces, 27″ × 34″ (68.58cm × 86.36cm).

71. Venturella, *St. Francis*, 293 pieces, 22″ × 46″ (55.88cm × 116.84cm). Details on hands, face, and feet require painting.

72. French, 156 pieces, 25″ × 27″ (63.5cm × 68.58cm).

73. Baum, 380 pieces, 27″ × 41″ (68.58cm × 104.14cm).

74. Cullenbine, *Red & Yellow Orchids*, 108 pieces, 32″ × 26″ (81.28cm × 66.04cm). If areas around flowers seem too difficult to cut as is, simplify by adding more lines.

75. French adaptation of comic book robot (Copyright © 1977 by D. C. Comics. All rights reserved), 232 pieces, 32″ × 48″ (81.28cm × 121.92cm).

76. Louis Comfort Tiffany, 753 pieces, 45″ × 28″ (114.30cm × 71.12cm). From window in the Kimmelman residence, New York, New York.

77. Mellen, border design and side light pattern.

Three-dimensional

78. French, 65 pieces, 10″ (25.4cm) measured flat from wing tip to tip. Reinforcement bars (shown above pattern) are soldered between wings to hold them in an upright position. Black areas indicate where to float solder.

79. Sell, (A) 29 pieces, enlarge central rectangle to 4″ × 7″ (10.16cm × 17.78cm) and the sides will be in correct proportion; (B) 21 pieces, enlarge central rectangle to 6″ × 4″ (15.24cm × 10.16cm); (C) 16 pieces, enlarge central rectangle to 6″ × 4″ (15.24cm × 10.16cm). Cut bottom piece after putting together sides. The bottom should be almost exactly the same size as the lid.

80. Nugget, 29 pieces, enlarge and measure one of the two blank side panels to 4 7/16″ × 5 5/16″ (11.28cm × 13.49cm) or take your measurements directly from a tall tissue box. Tissue boxes do not require bottom sections. Shading indicates tissue opening.

81. Nugget, 28 pieces, enlarge lid of box to 8.9″ × 6″ (22.86cm × 15.24cm). Lid is meant to be larger than the box it covers.

82. Mellen, 185 pieces, enlarge central rectangle to 17″ × 13″ (43.18cm × 33.02cm) and sides will be in correct proportion. When soldering together this pattern, attach the four sides at a 90-degree angle to the front section. This will give the mirror a box shape that stands away from the wall when hung.

83. French, 72 pieces (12 large and 60 small border pieces). Cut pattern to size. First put together the separate polygon shapes, 10 in all, and then put these shapes together to form the terrarium. One polygon shape should be hinged.

84. French, 486 pieces, enlarge dotted line to 10″ (25.4cm). The lamp is a simple repeat and reverse design from a single pattern. Considering the size of this project, make sure that you are comfortable with panel lamp construction before undertaking the project.

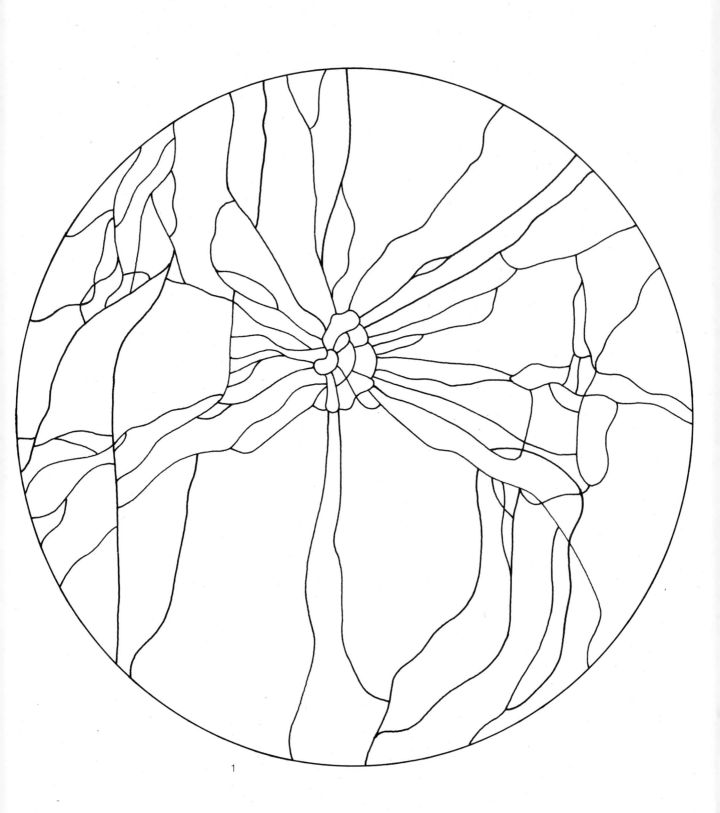

1

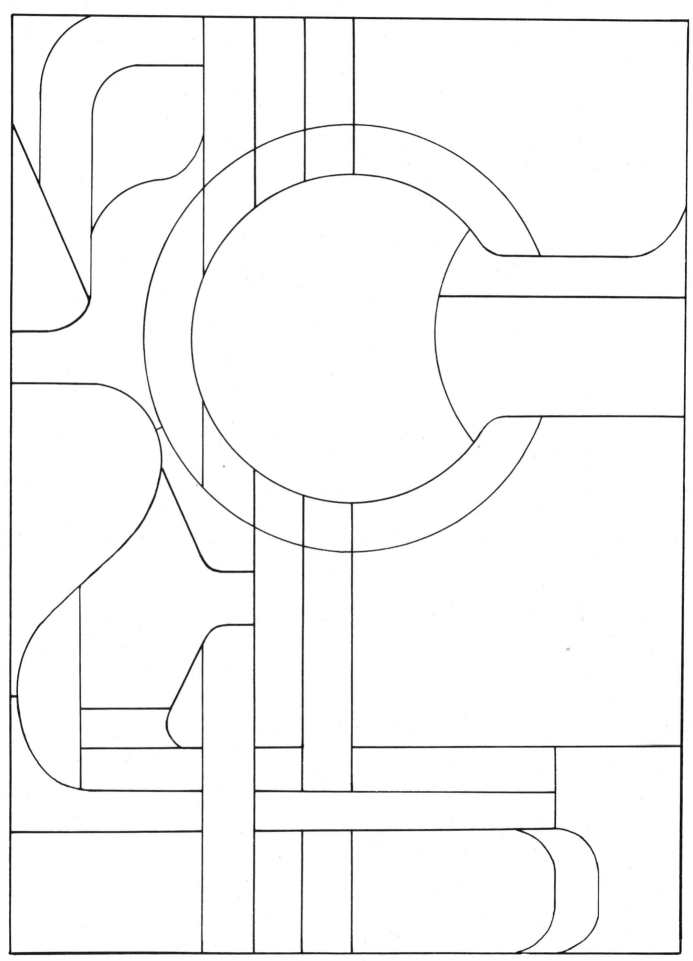

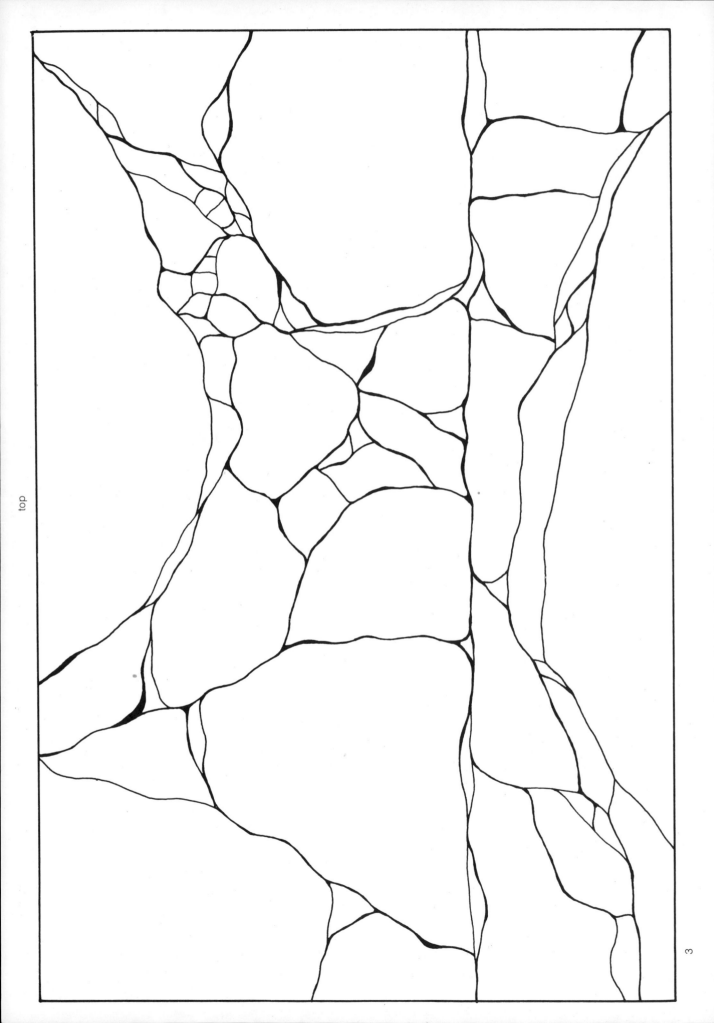

4

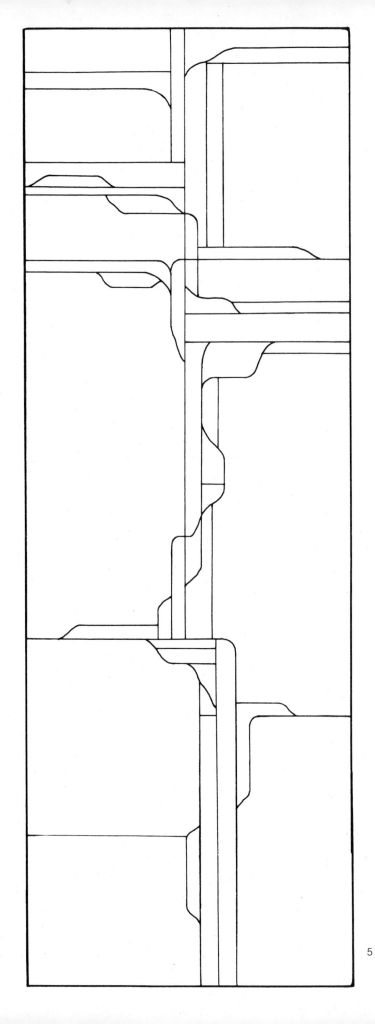

5

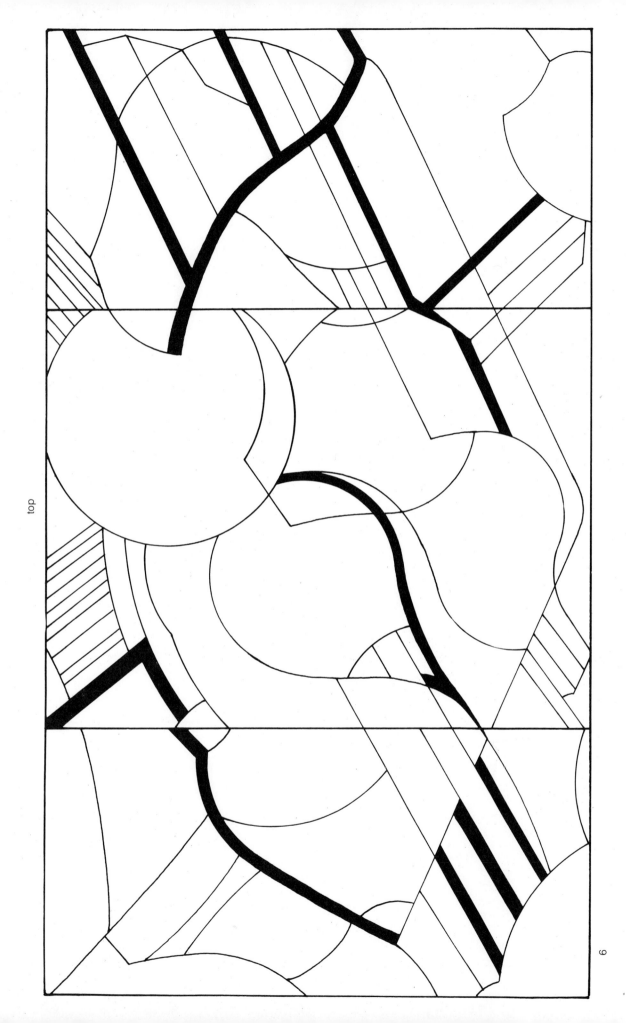

top

6

7

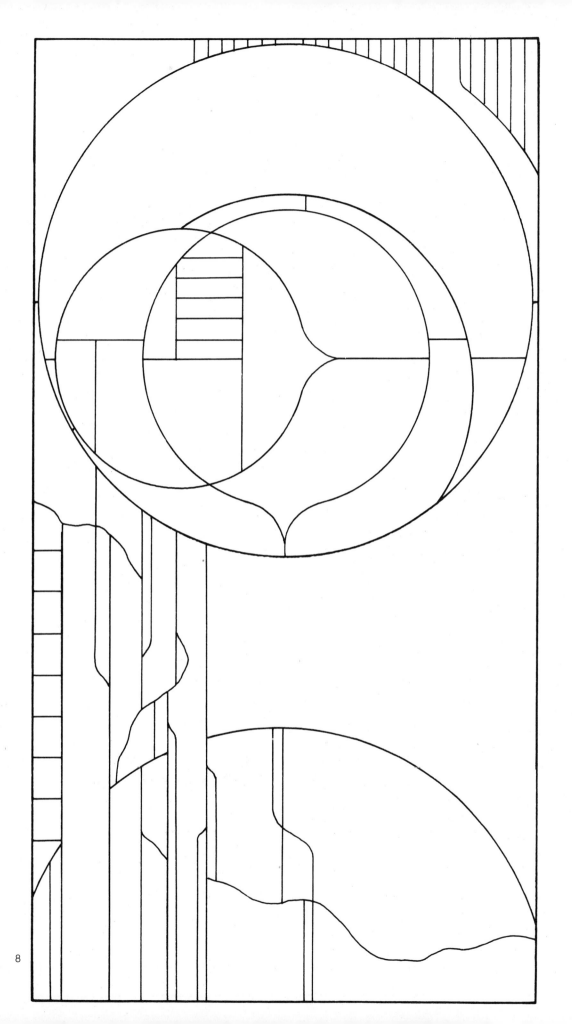

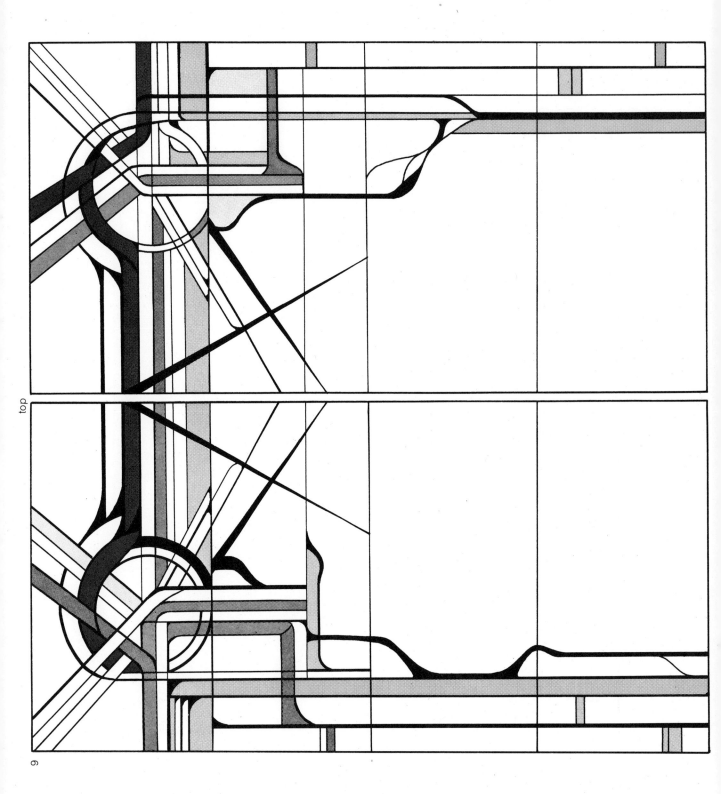

6

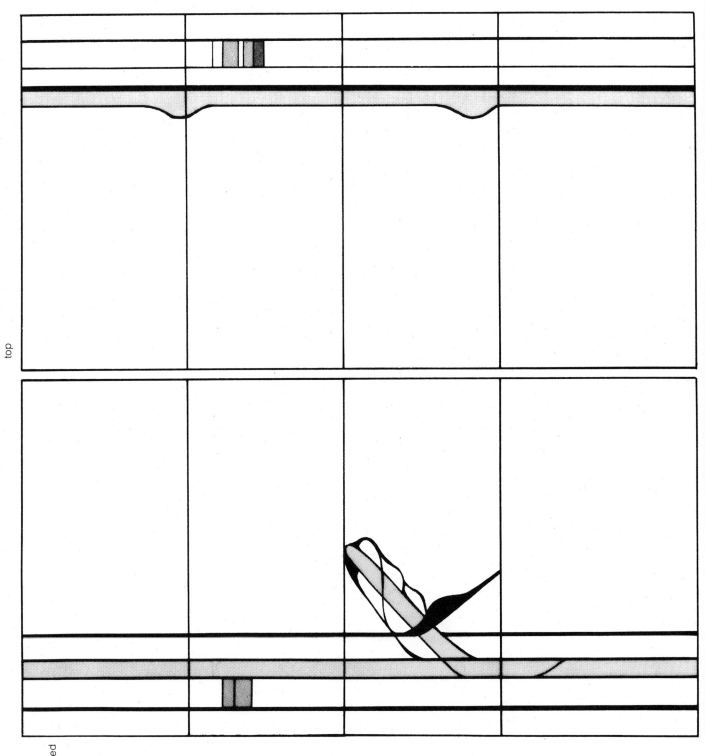

10

11

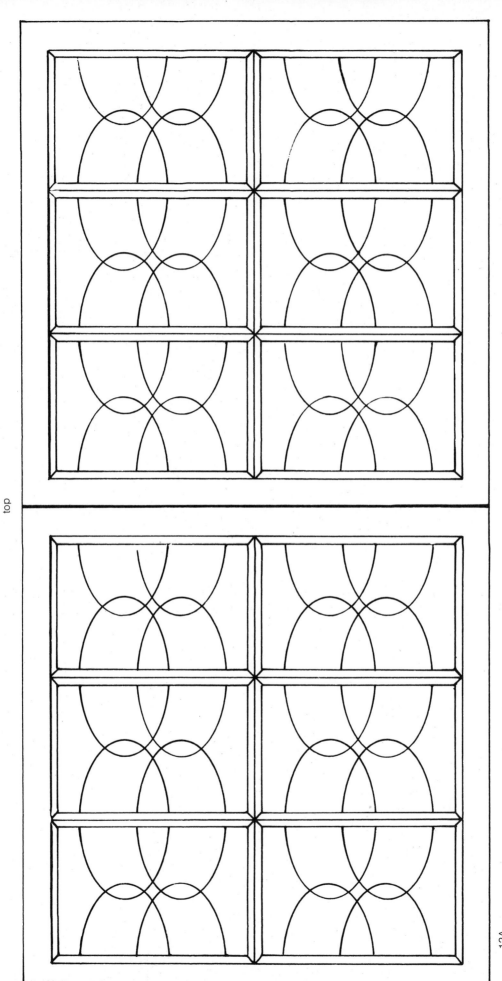

top

12A

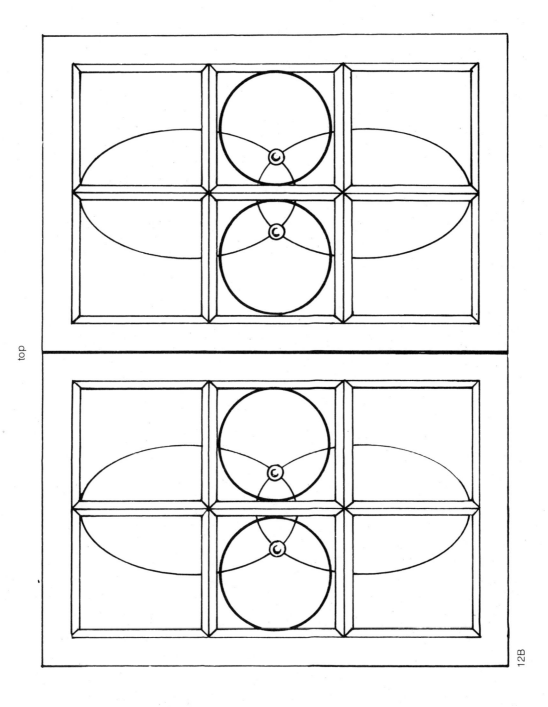

12B

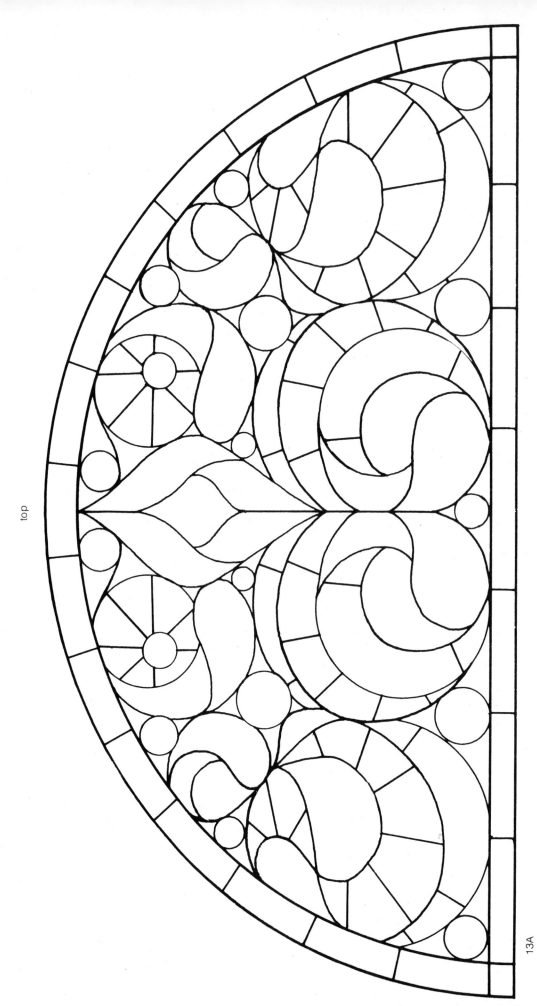

top

13A

46

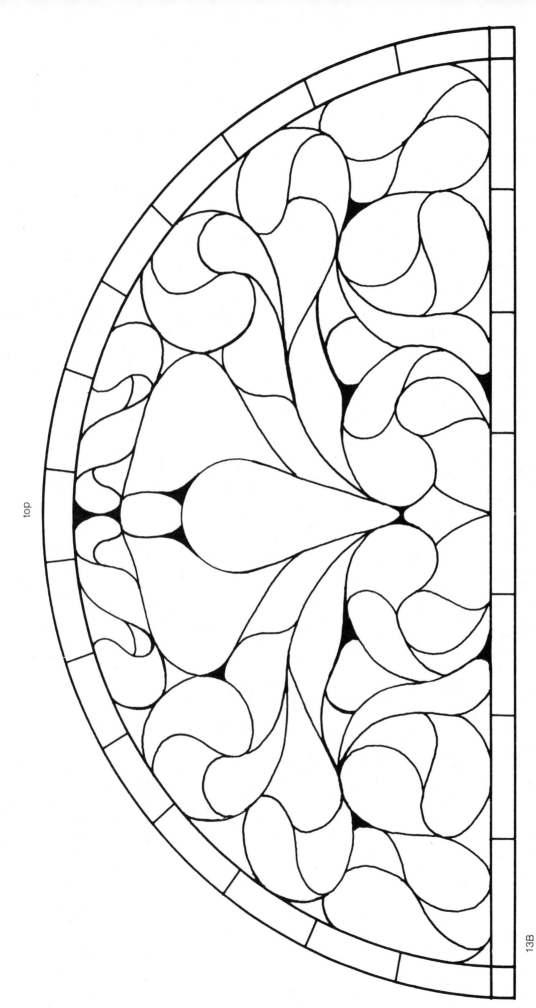

top

13B

14

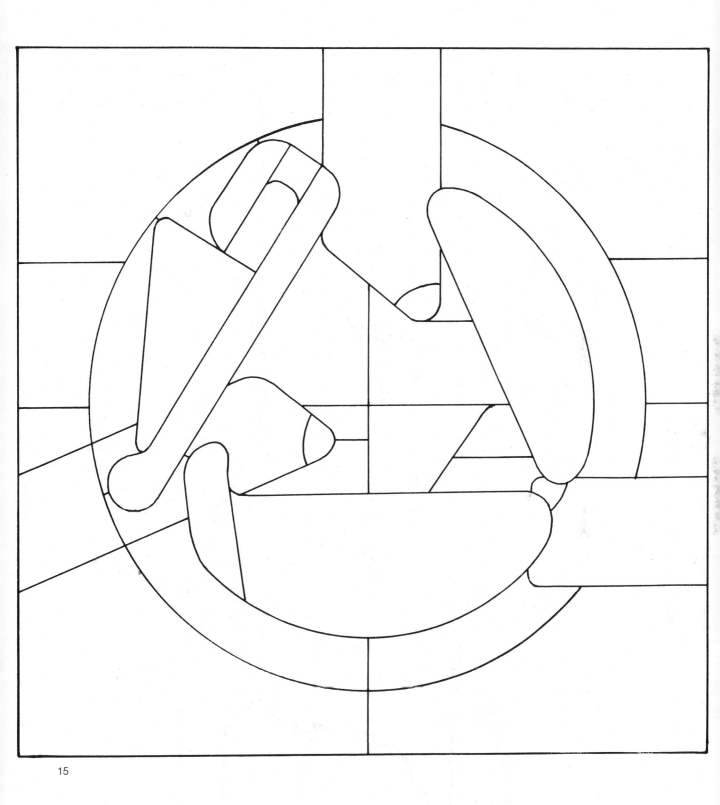

15

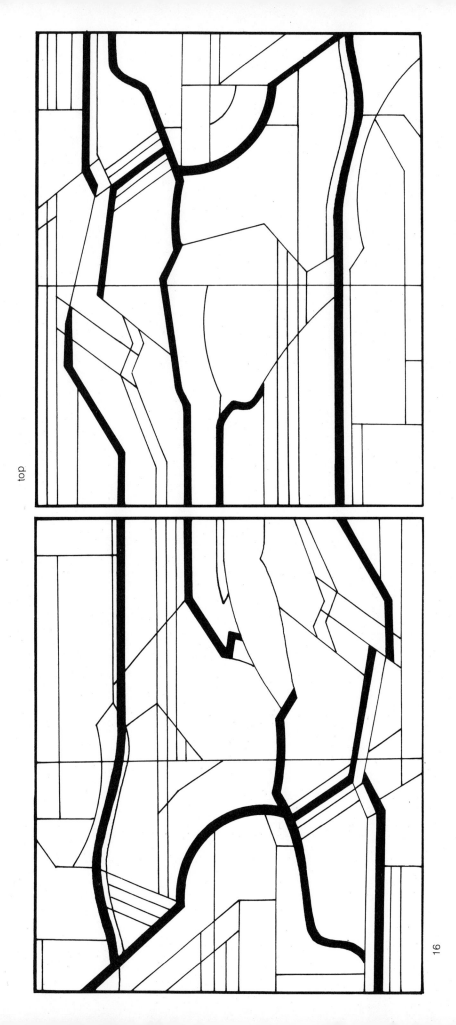

top

16

50

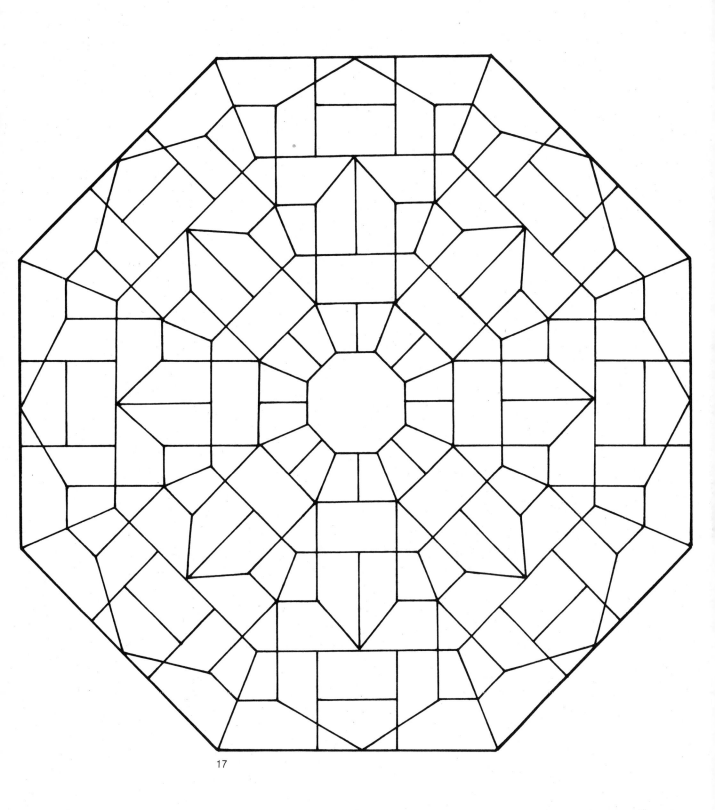

17

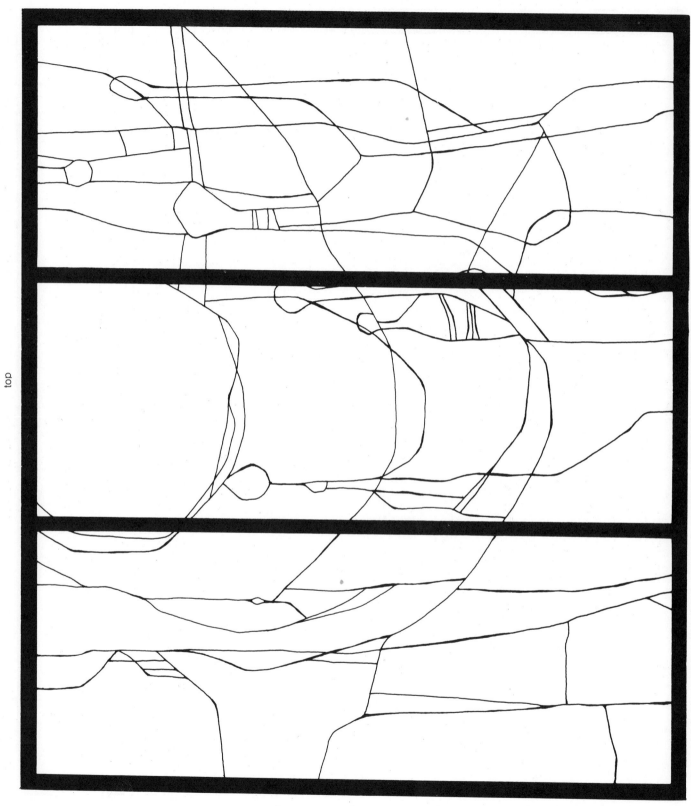

top

19

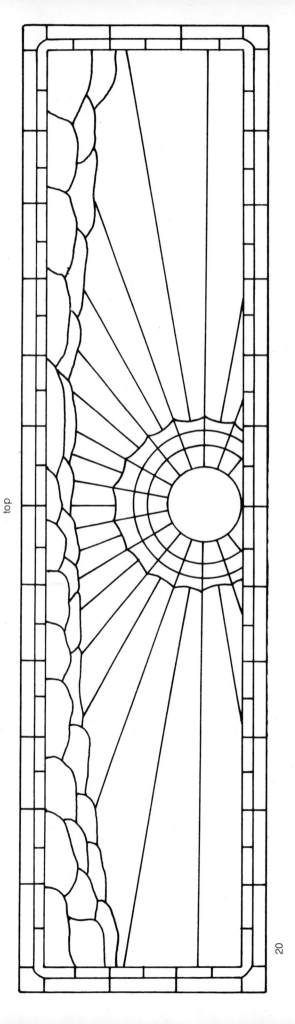

top

20

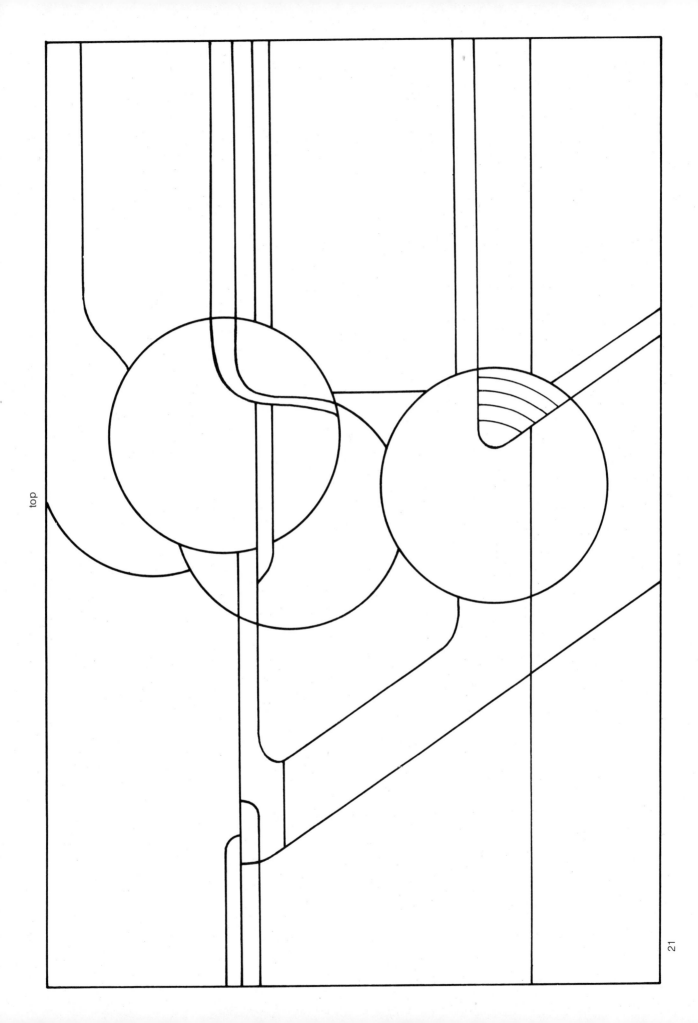

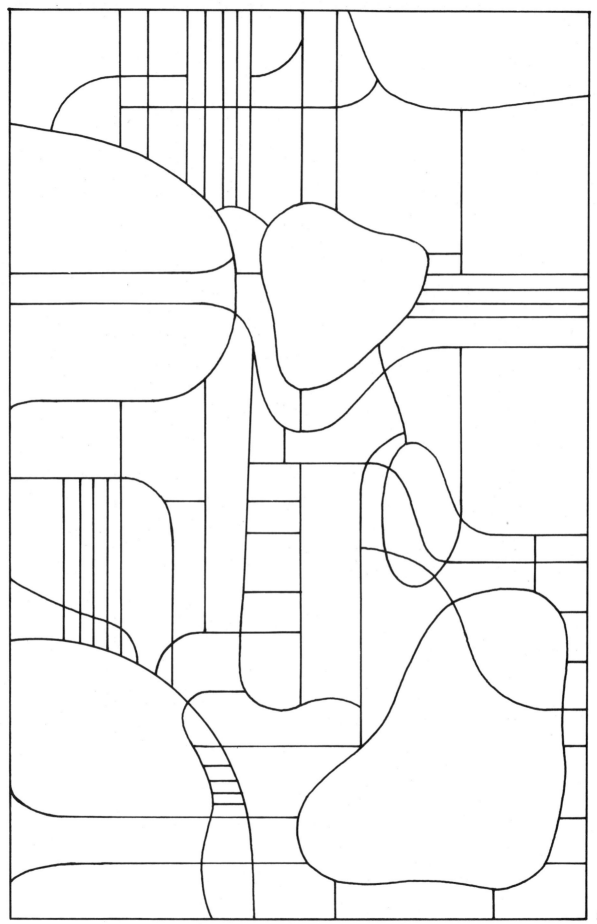

22

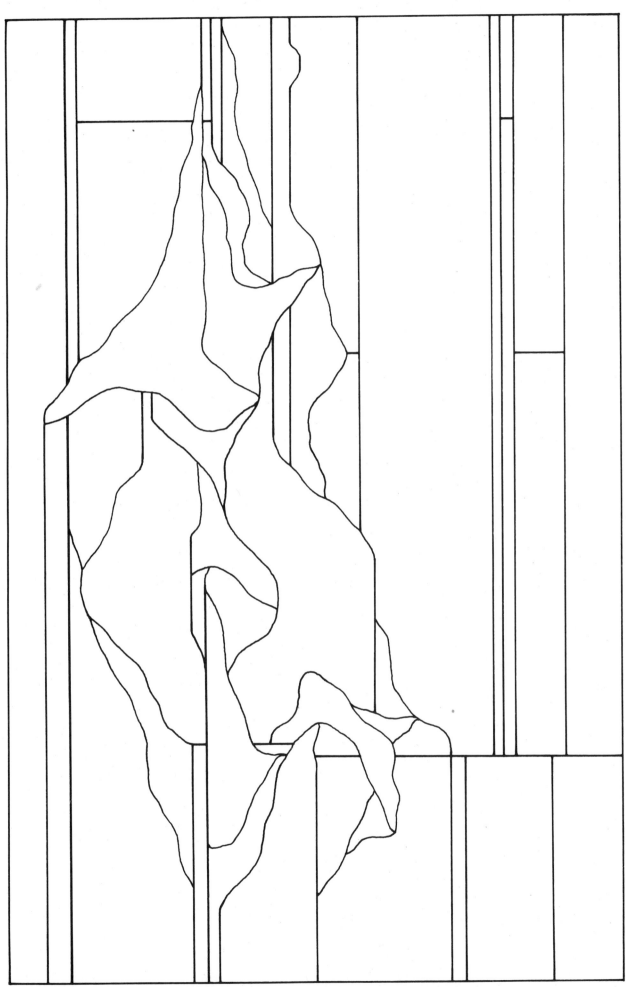

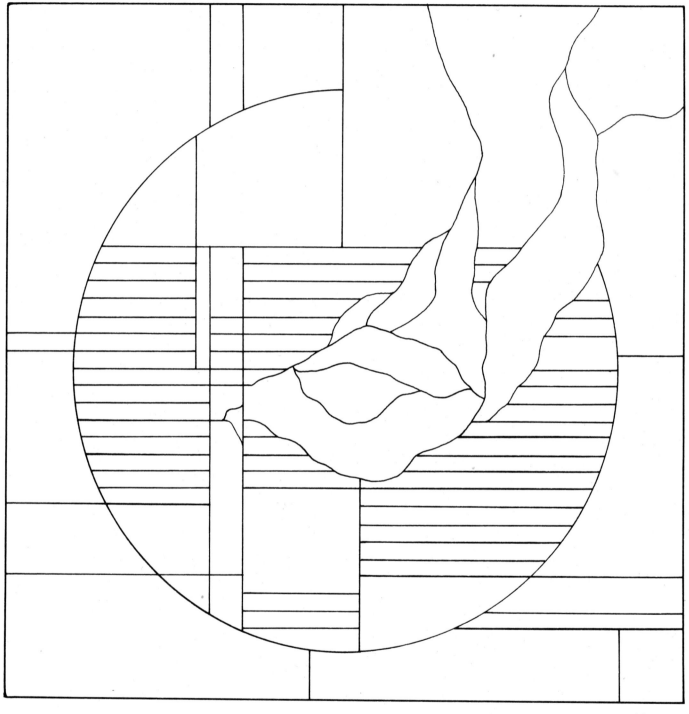

24

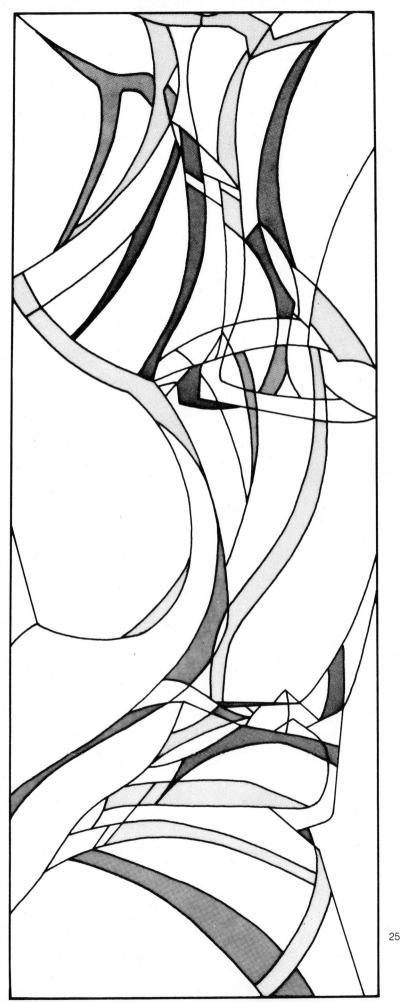

25

26

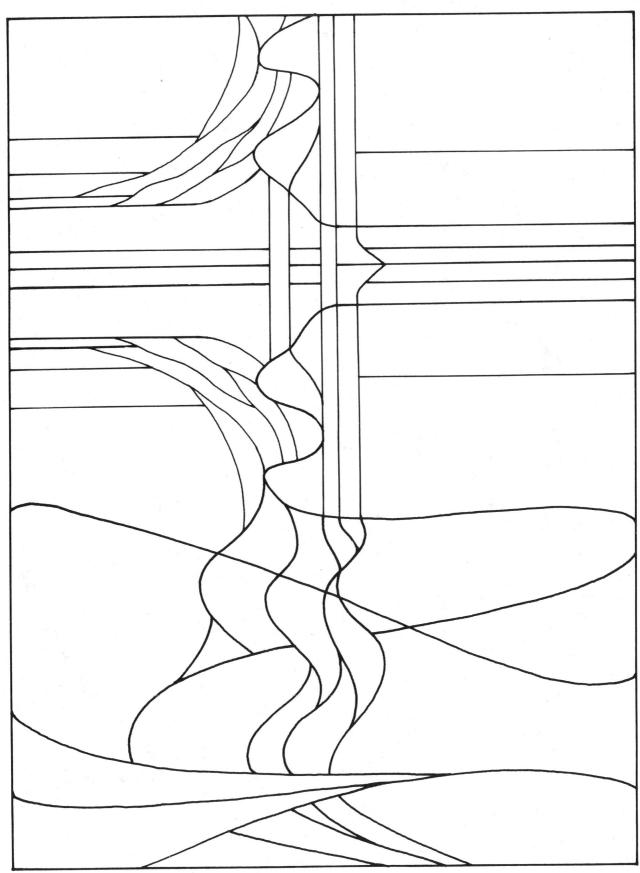

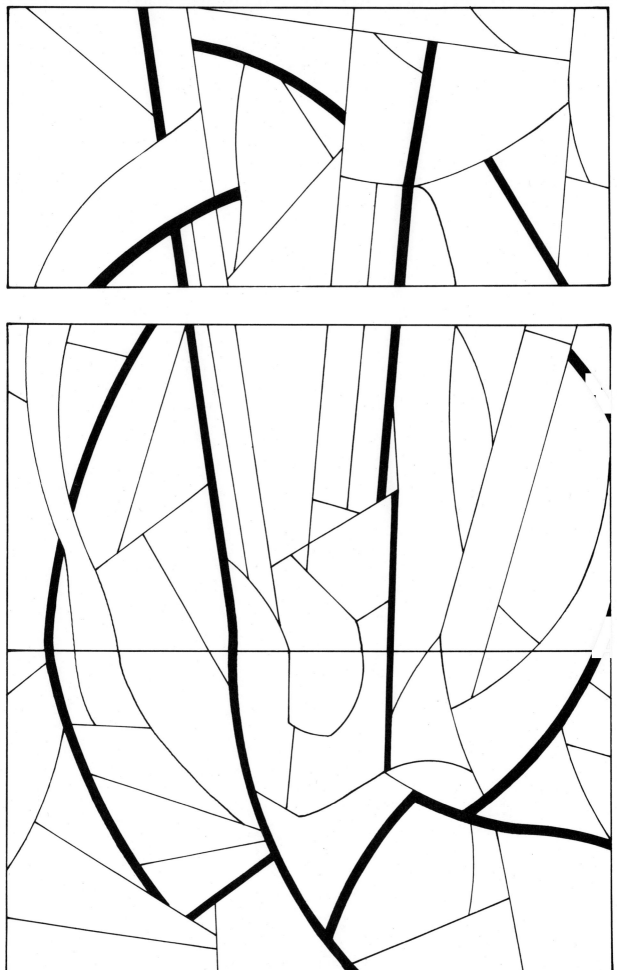

top

28

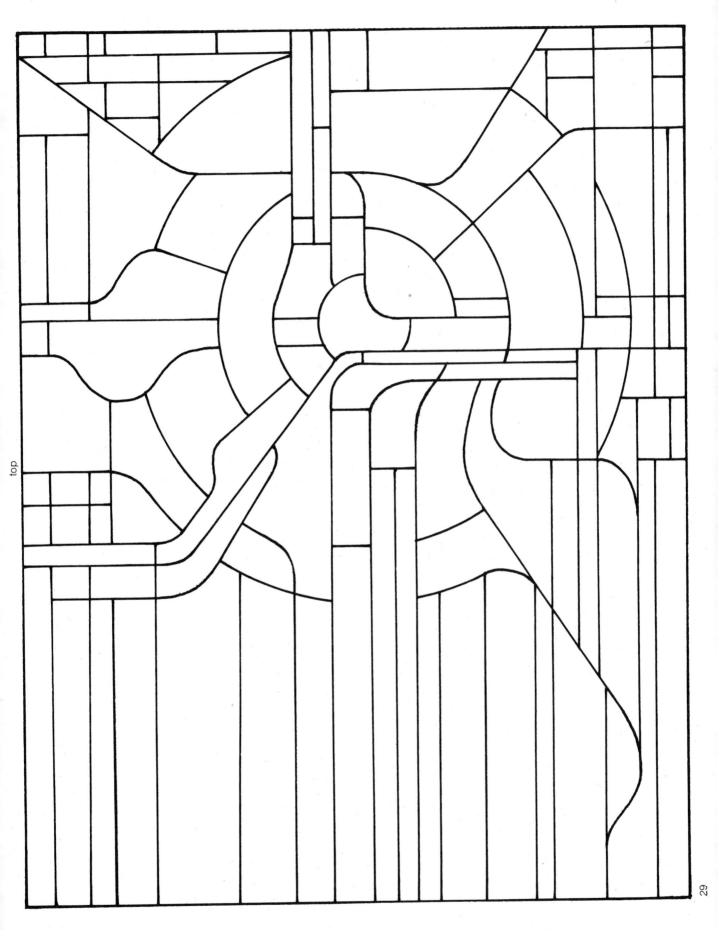

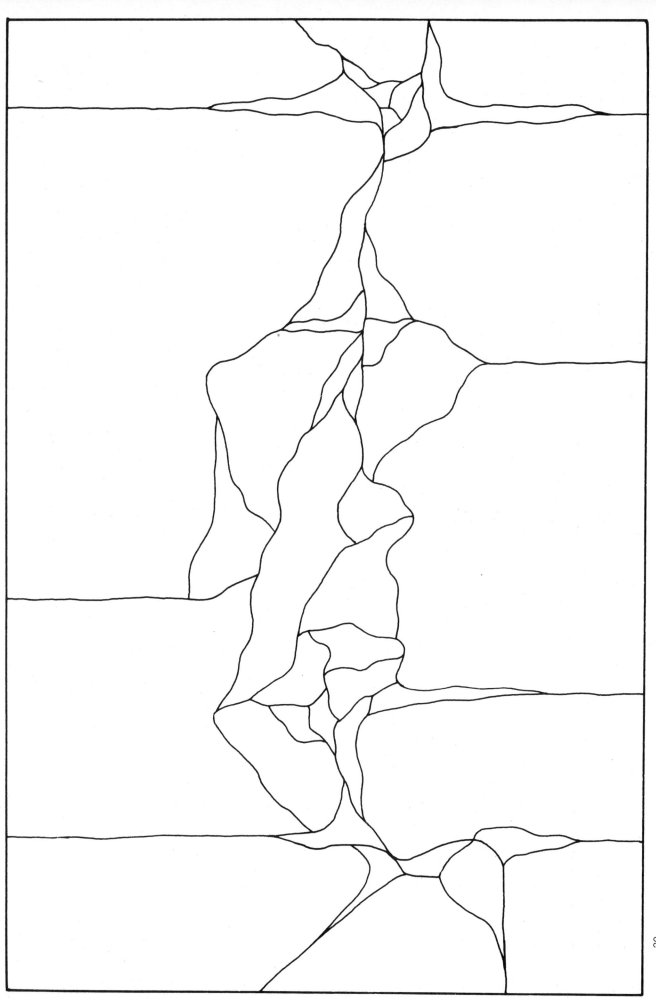

31

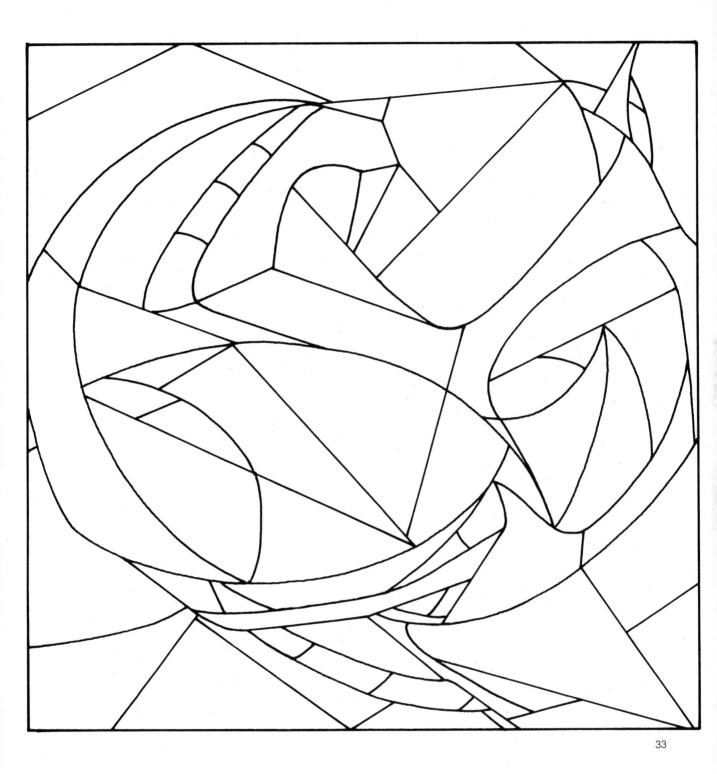

33

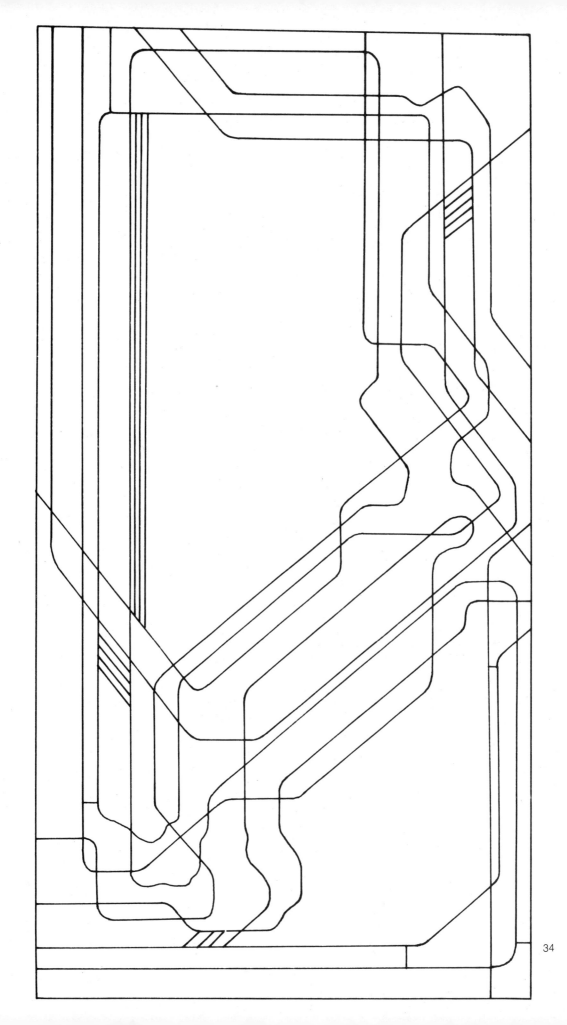

34

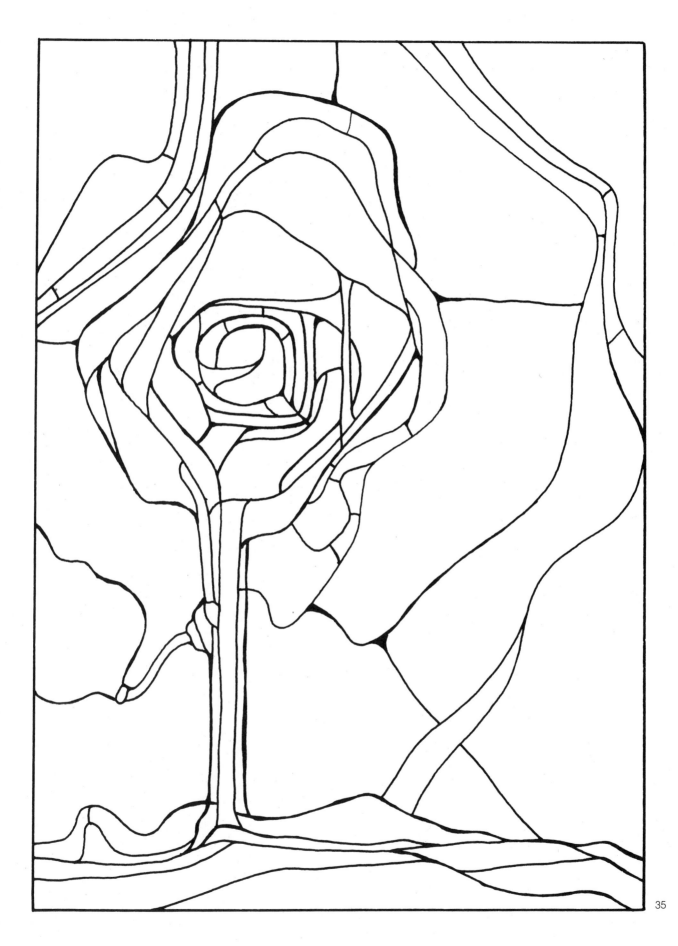

35

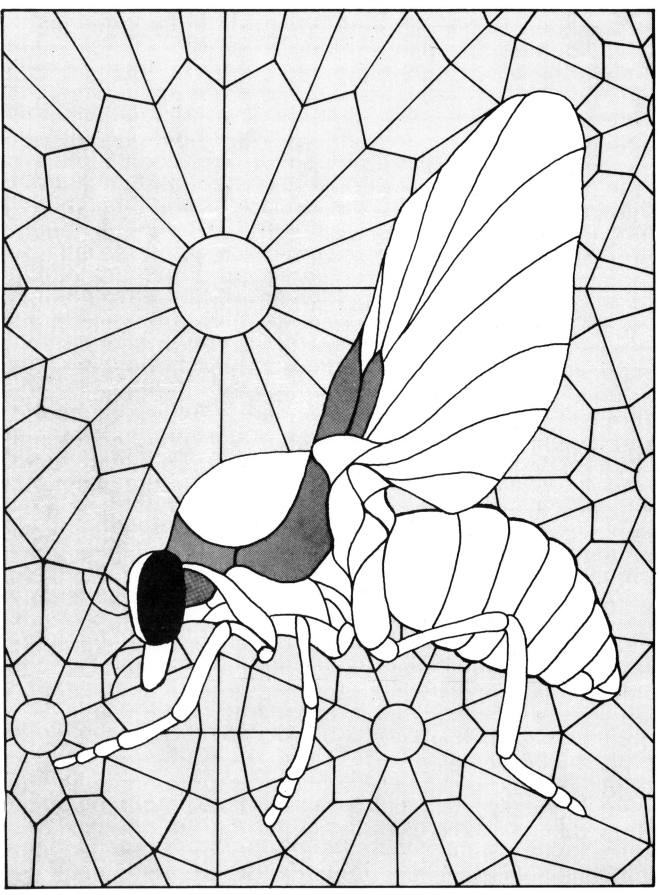

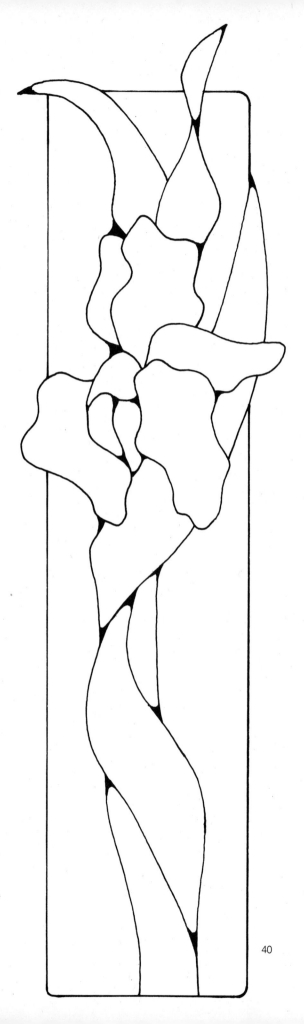

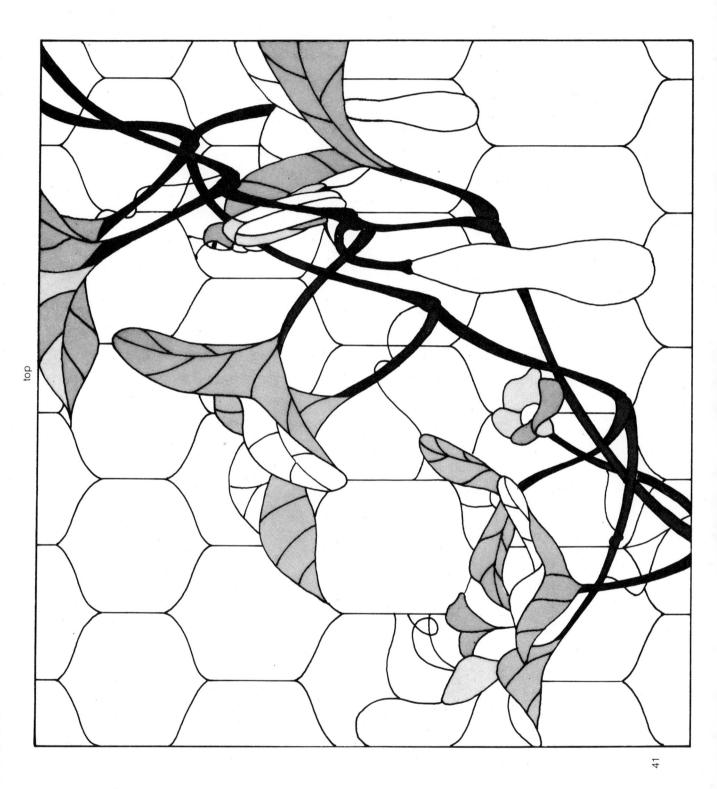

top

42

top

43

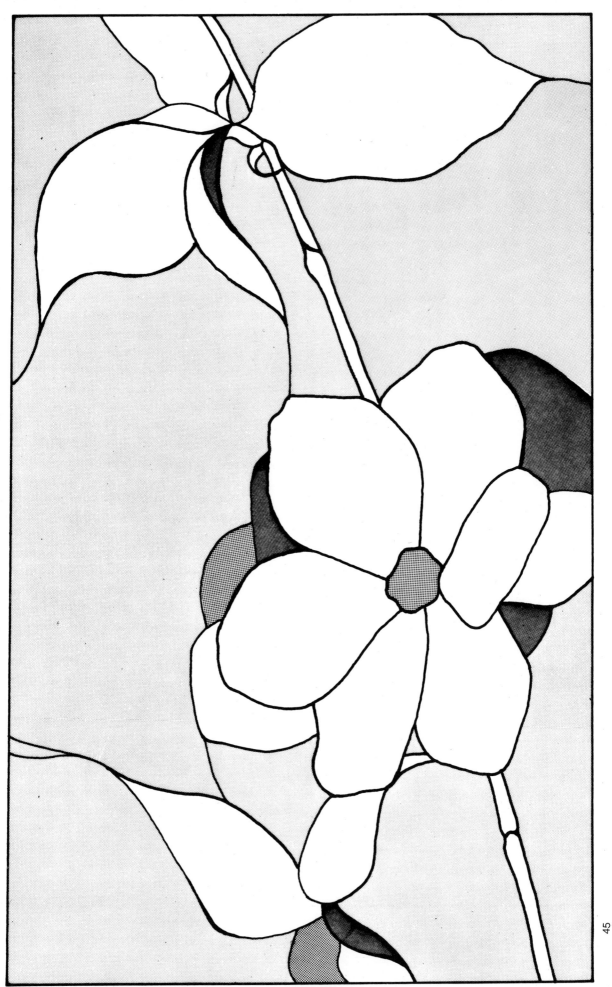

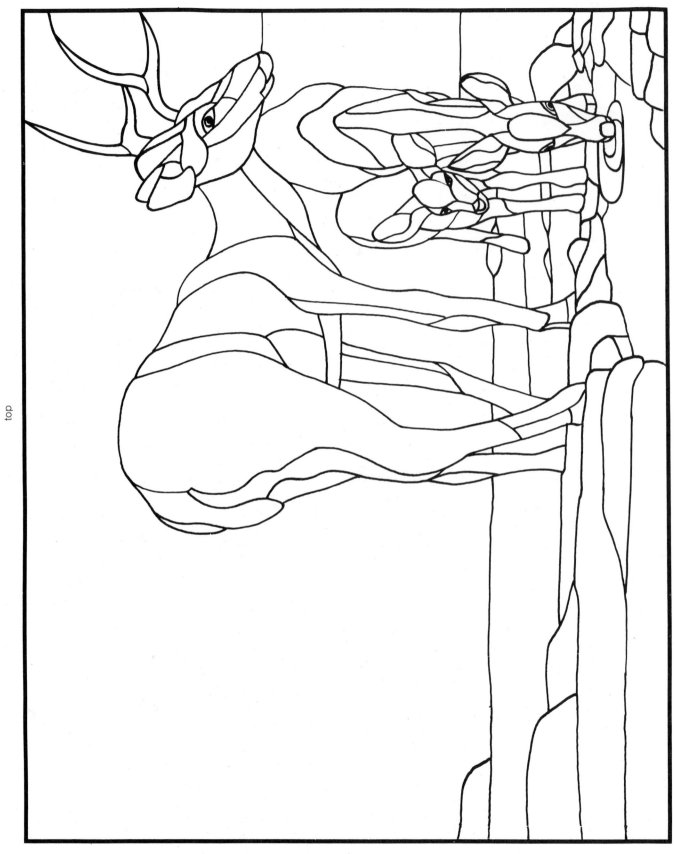

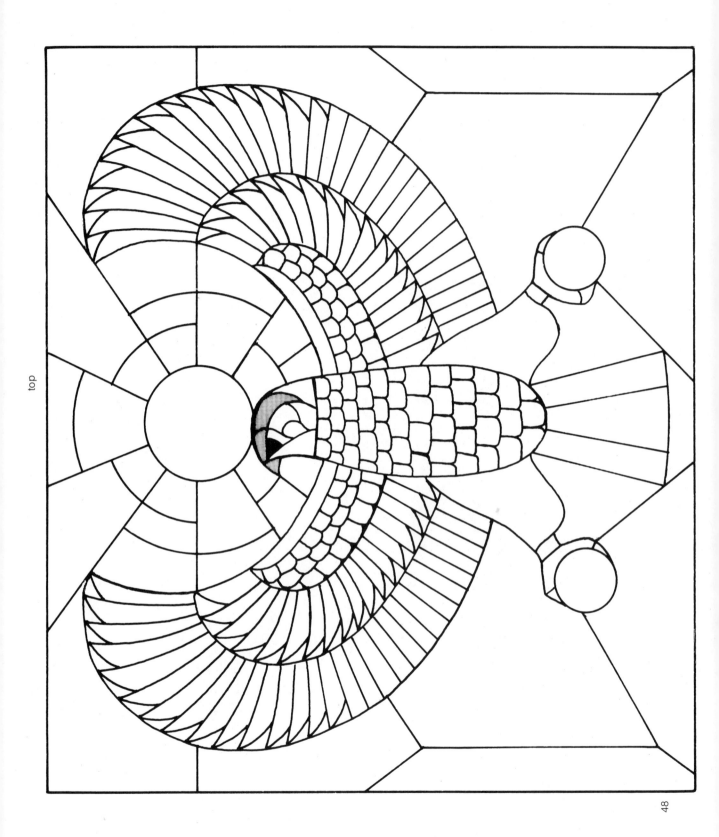

49

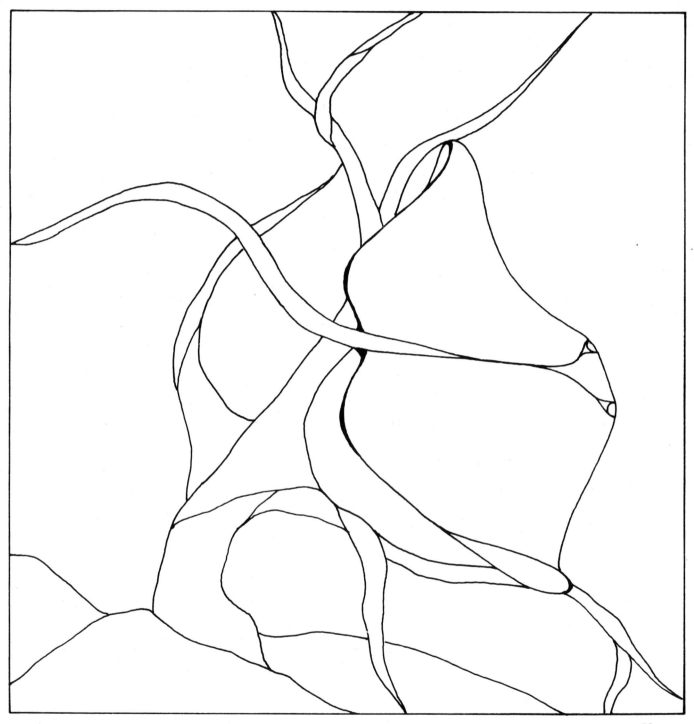

52

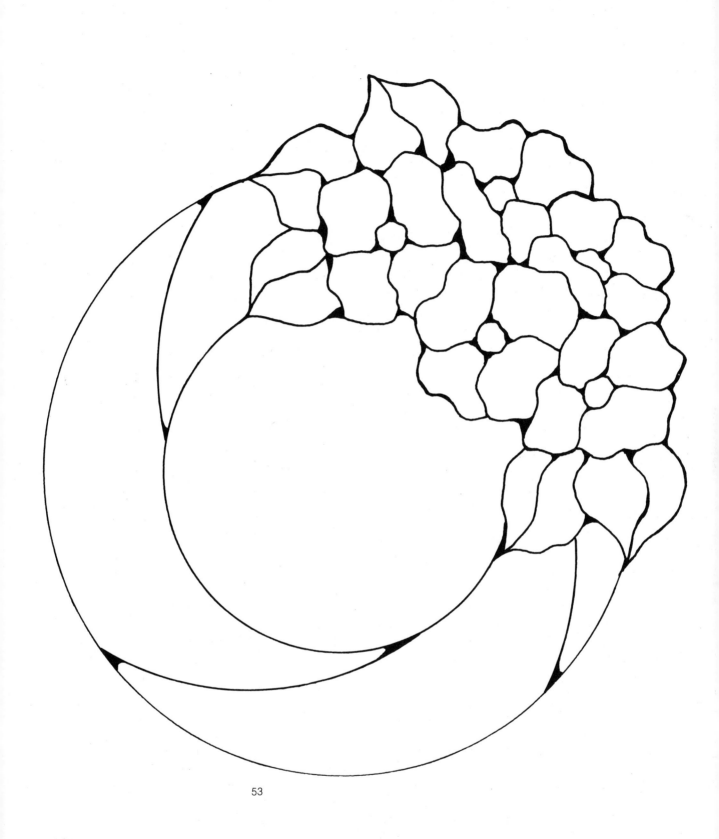

53

55

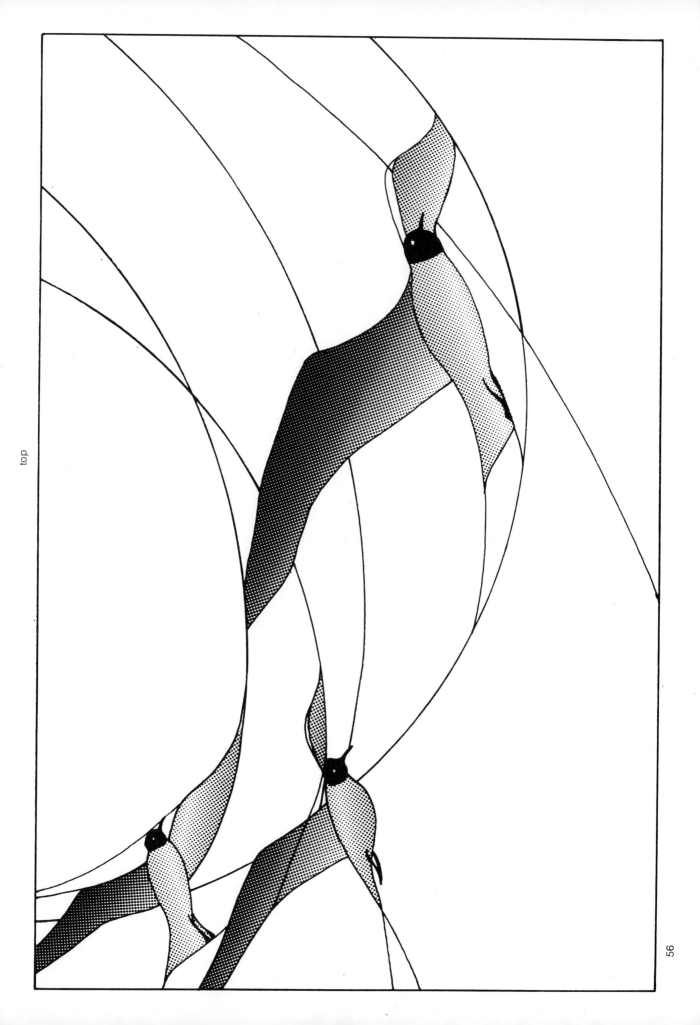

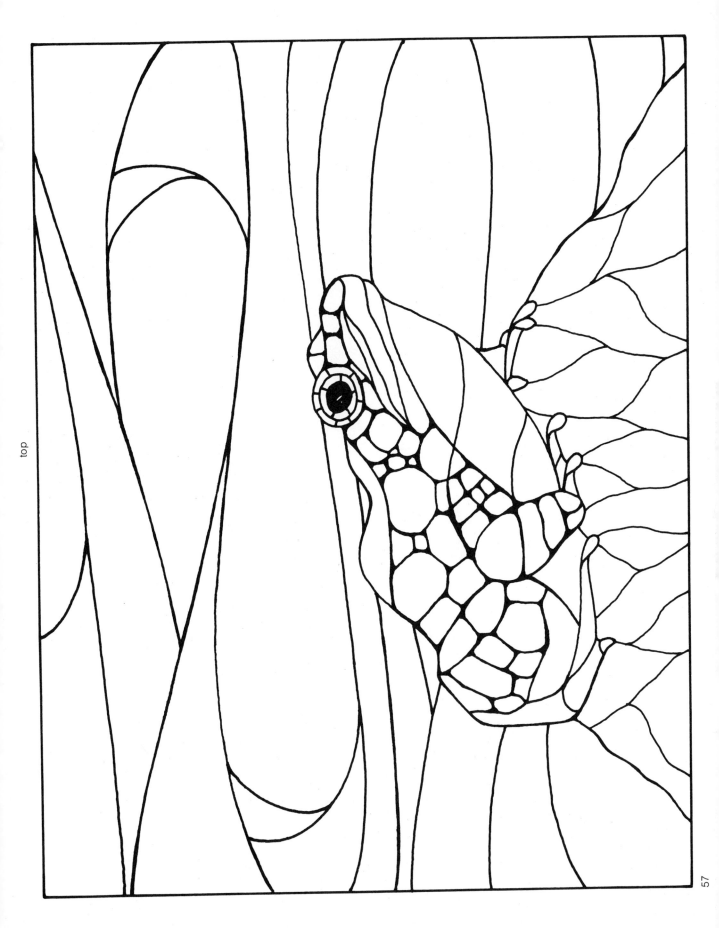

59

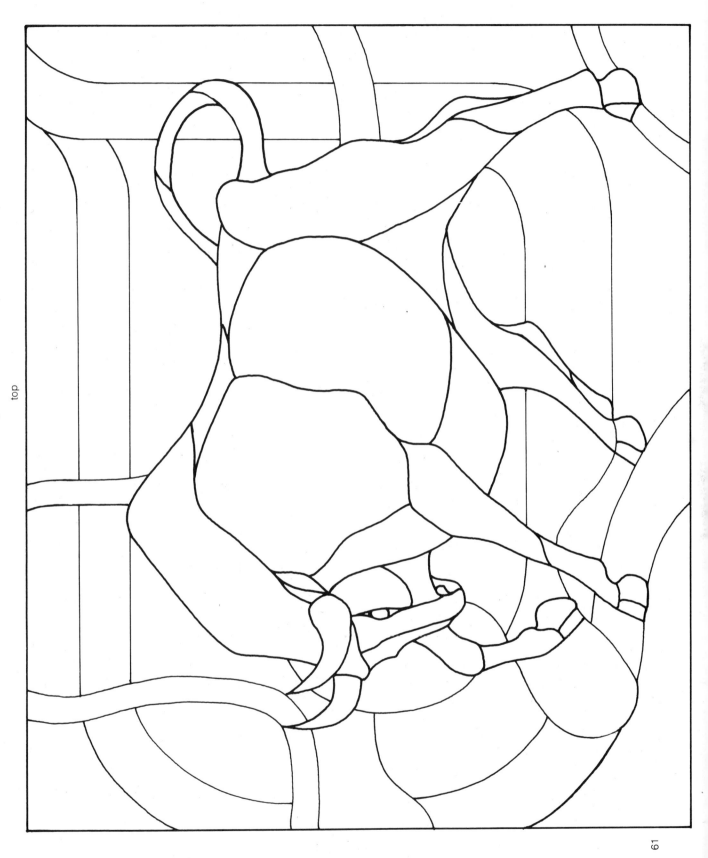

64

70

71

73

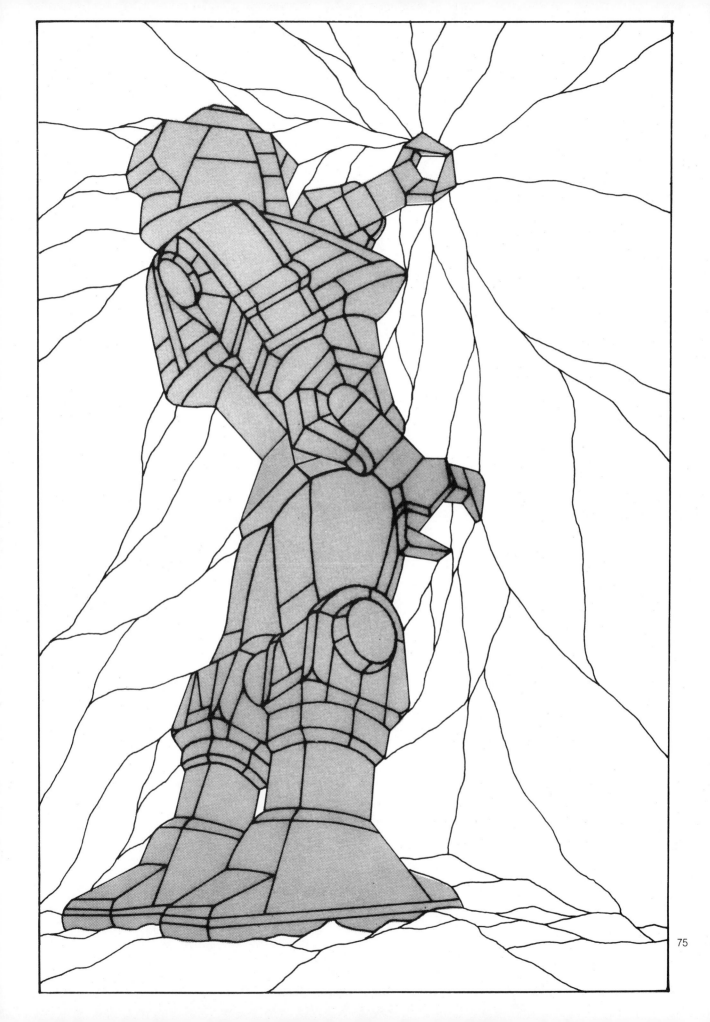

75

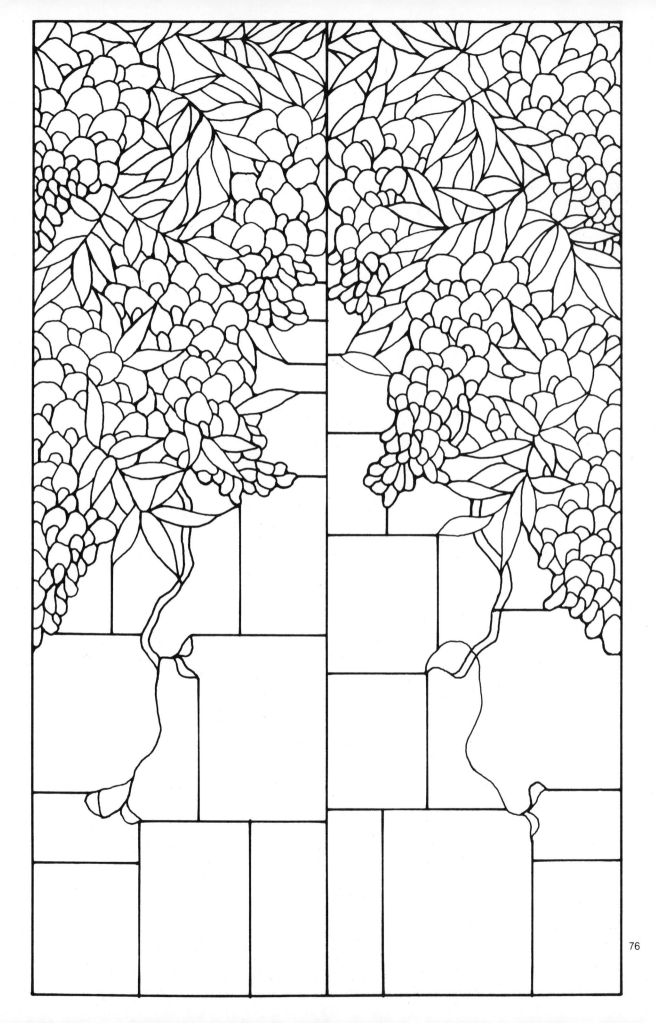

77

78

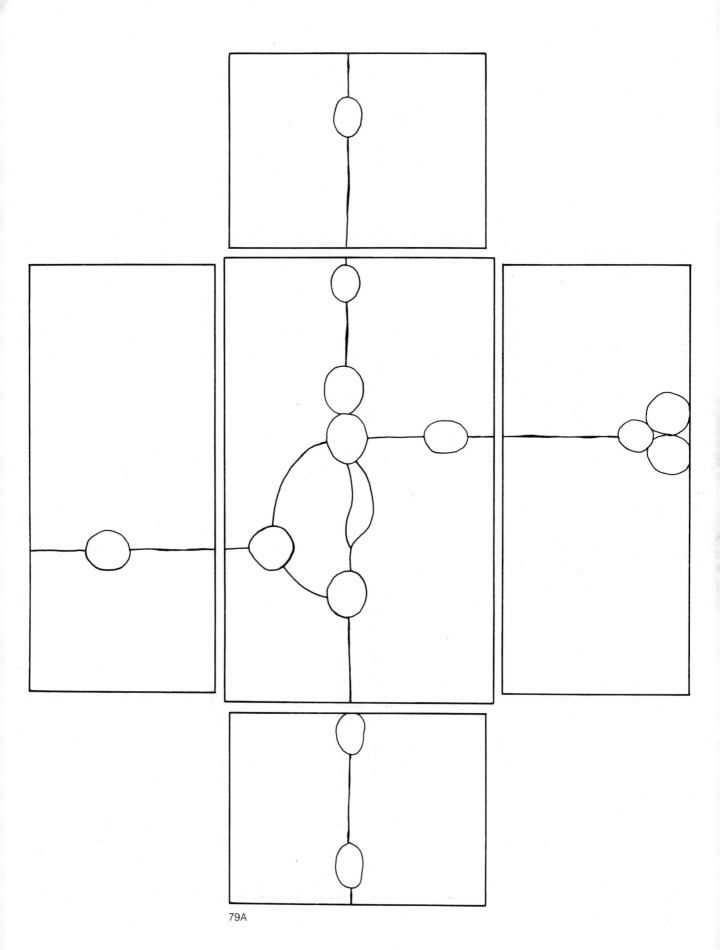

79A

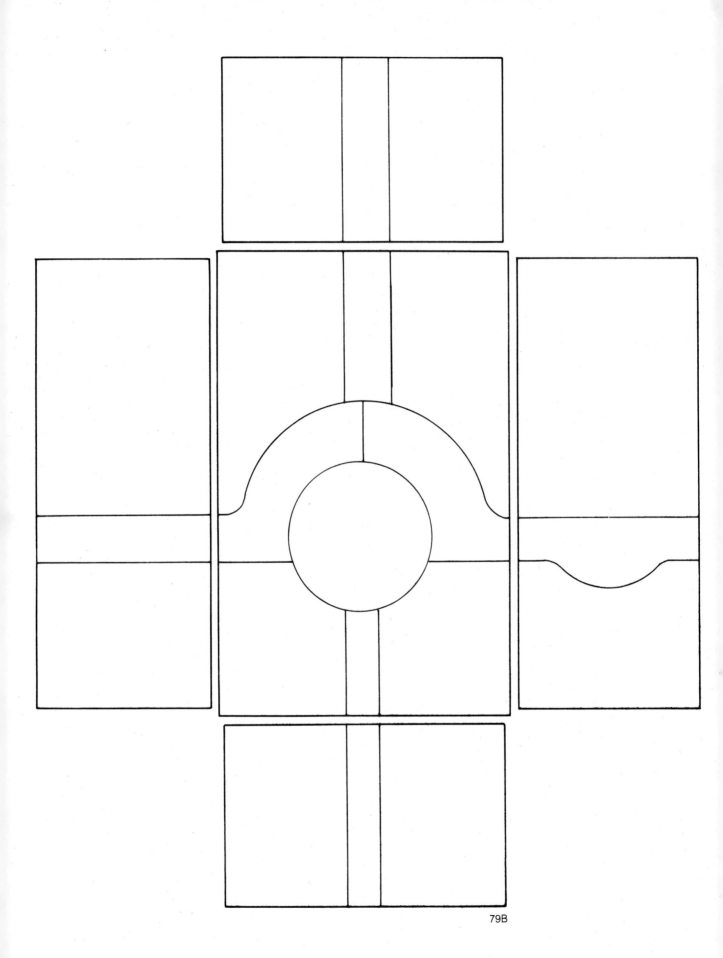

79B

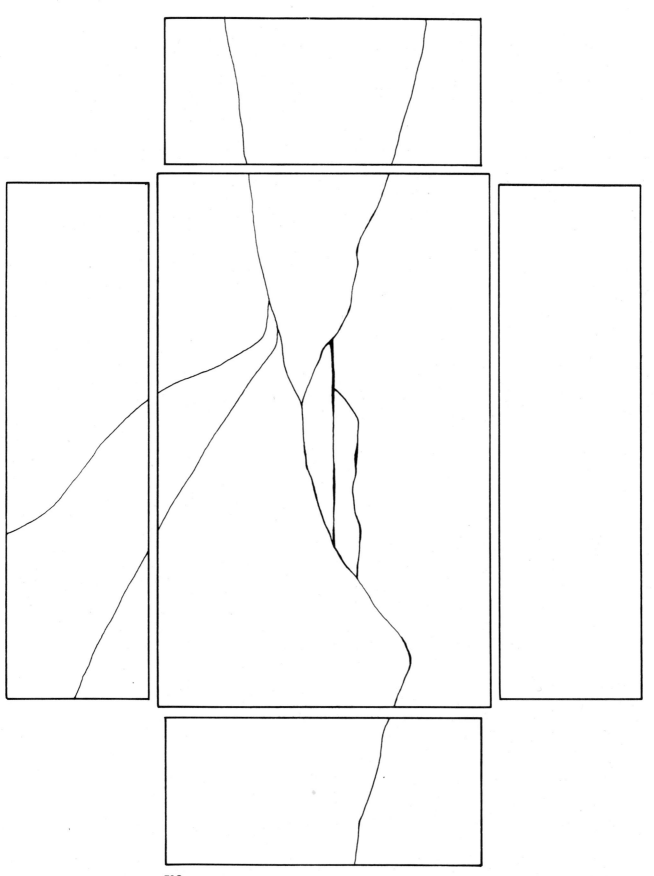

79C

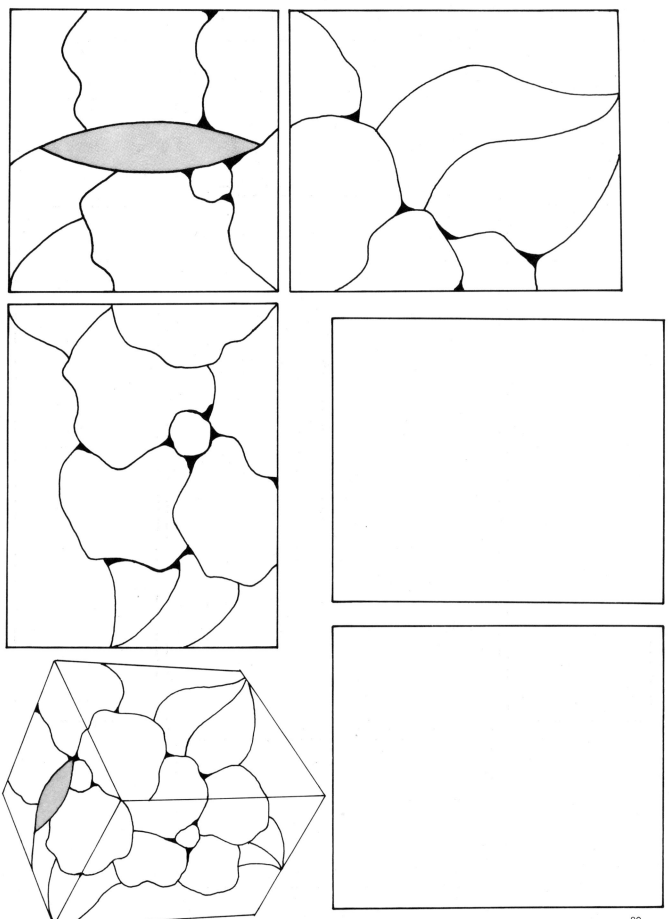

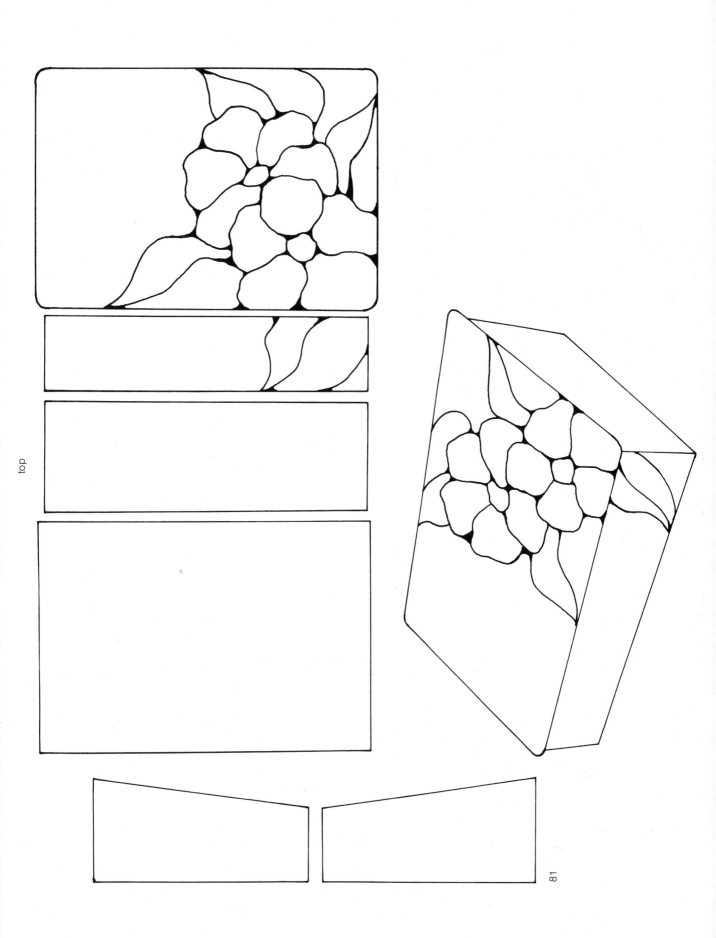

81

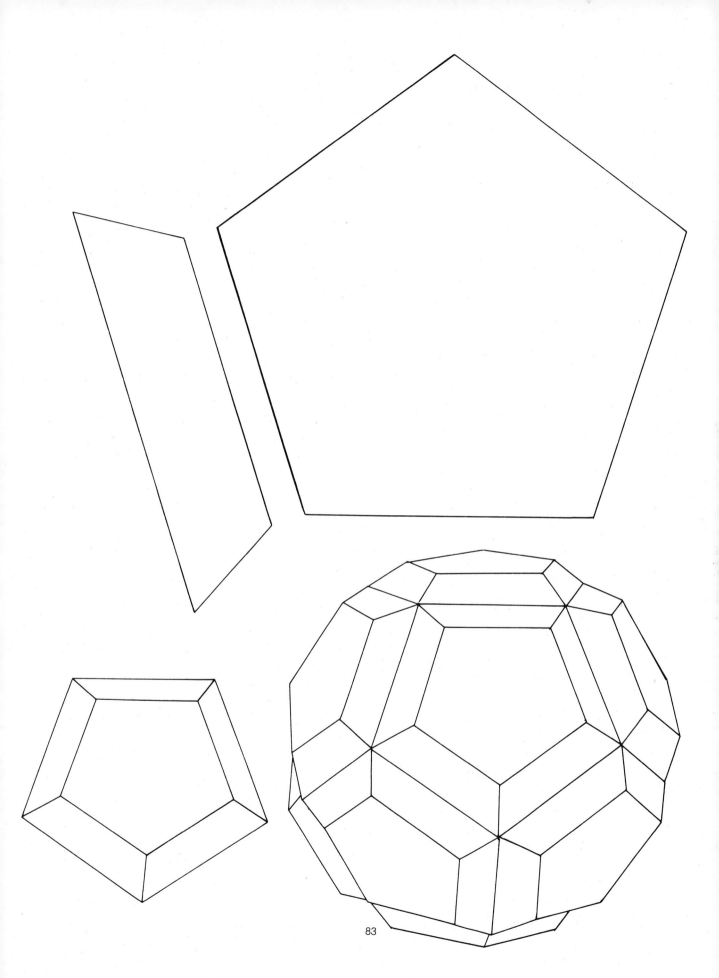

83

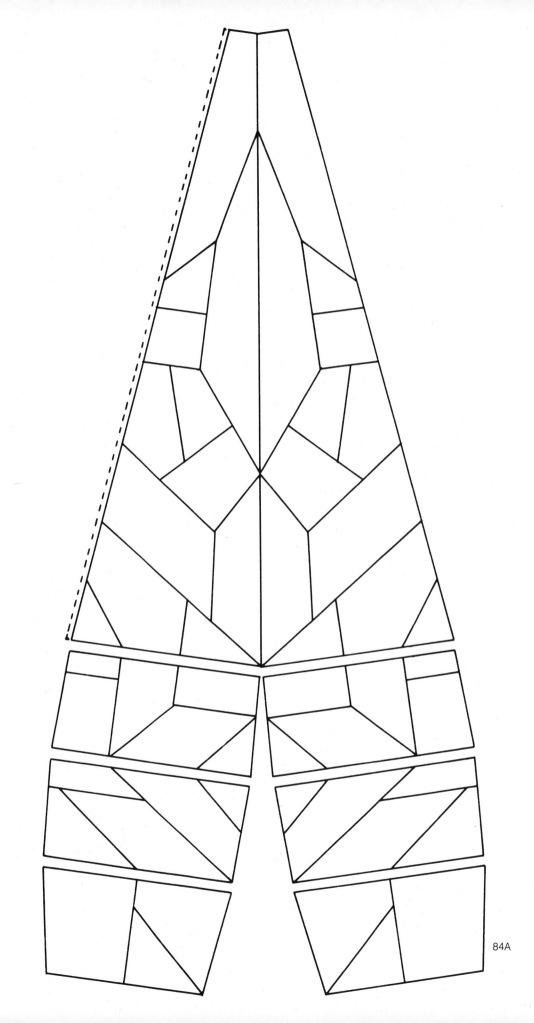

84A

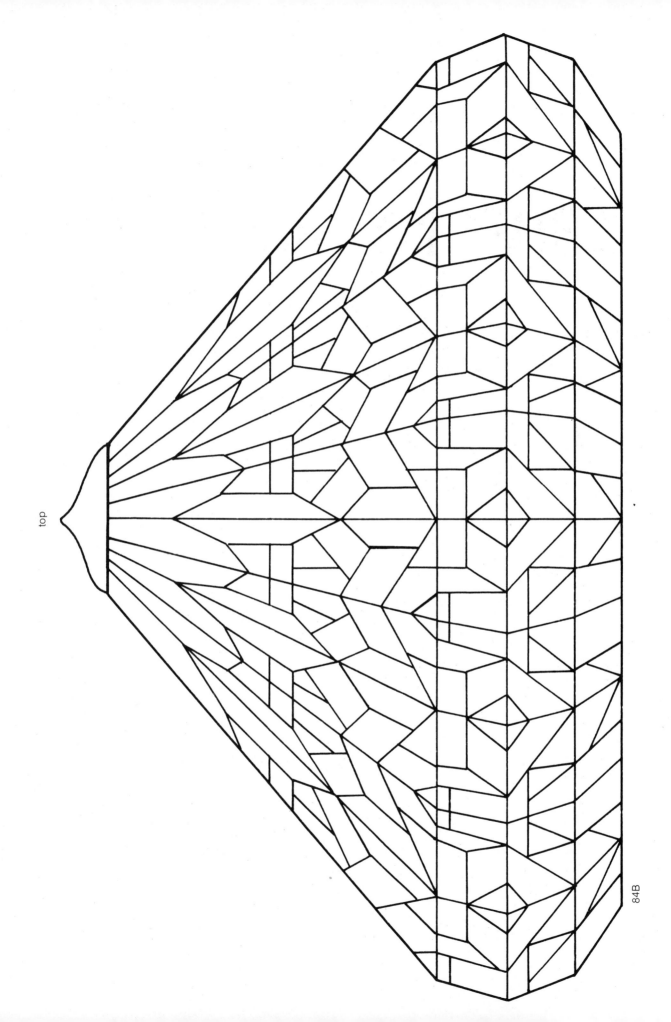

top

84B

3.

CRAFT INSTRUCTION

Structure: Flat work

The differences between lead came and copperfoil work extend far beyond the cosmetic appearance of the line. The most important factors that insure the solidity of lead came work are the leading sequence and the reinforcement or bracing of the work. This must be considered in the initial planning stage, whereas, due to the nature of the technique, copperfoil work is naturally quite strong. It forms an interlocking, hard metal web structure that requires a minimum of reinforcement when done well.

Some similarities between the two techniques, however, do exist and are worth mentioning. The pieces of glass and lead that make up a design are individual units or bits of weight that are subjected to at least two quietly violent forces: gravity and weather (or temperature) changes. Gravity exerts a slow. crushing pull that is powerful enough to crack glass over a period of time or buckle a poor leading job and leave the glass dangling in its framework. This process is aided by weather changes. Imagine the punishment delivered to an exterior window by wind, rain, freezing temperatures, and a baking sun. Even the subtle climatic changes that occur indoors have a cumulative effect on glass, causing it to contract and expand minutely.

A thorough study of structure takes more than a few pages but if you can grasp the basic concept, time and experience can then take over as your guide. What you must try to achieve is an even distribution of weights and stresses throughout a design, much as an architect does when designing a building.

The two areas in flat work where most people run into difficulty are in not considering the physical weight of glass and lead and in allowing lead lines to travel uninterrupted from edge to edge in any direction (horizontal, angled, or curved). The exception to this rule is uninterrupted vertical lead lines, which often help to strengthen the design.

Both problems are solved by adding supportive lead lines and/or reinforcement work.

Structure is immediately strengthened whenever a line is intercepted by another line. The new line or lines can take any shape and direction that is compatible with the rest of the design and need not dramatically alter the design unless a new color is introduced, (fig. 3–1).

A related problem occurs when the physical bulk of a design is placed too far off to one single area. This area becomes vulnerable and must be strongly reinforced. Unless the window or panel is reinforced, it can literally fold up where the two different weights are joined (fig. 3–2) or the area may buckle. Again, having lines intercept each other will strengthen the design. Depending on the size of the work, a few lines brought from the area of concentrated leading through less congested areas will spread the weight more evenly. Adding more lead lines may be a sufficient solution for a particular design but, when you do not want to alter your work or when even after such an alteration the design is still not strong, it becomes necessary to add reinforcement. In fact, except for small designs meant to dangle in windows, it is required. Reinforcement is not the cure-all that makes weak designing permissible nor is it to be used in a desperate attempt to save your work. It is an everyday, integral part of the craft.

3-1 *Left*, the original design which is structurally weak; *center*, how the design can be strengthened without changing the overall appearance; *right*, the same lines of correction, but this time the colors have been changed and the design, therefore, looks quite different.

3-2. Three examples of poorly balanced designs and how this type of work folds up along the line where the two disparate weights meet.

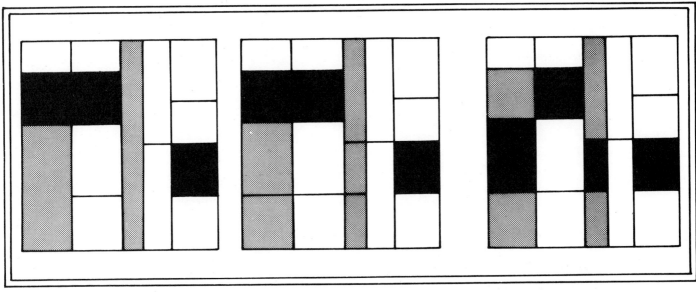

3-1

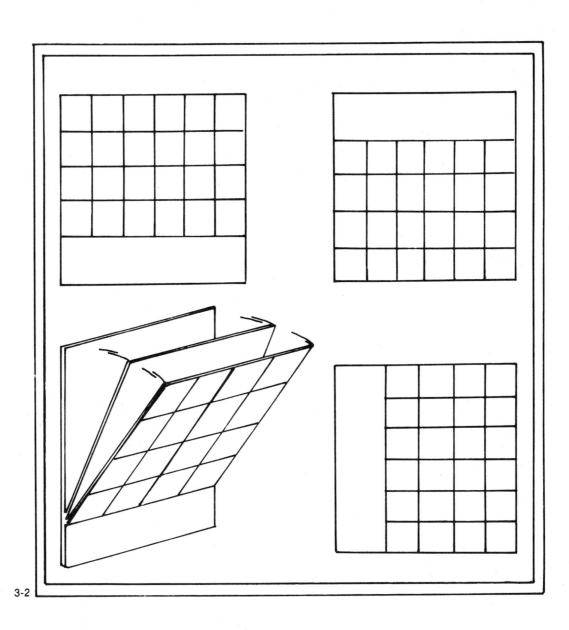

3-2

There are no strict rules to follow when reinforcing a glass panel but there are some generalities. If the body or perimeter of the work seems weak, then interior and perimeter lines will have to be reinforced. There are also certain installations that require the reinforcement work to extend beyond the perimeter, such as window panels intended for swinging doors or large, free-hanging panels. In these cases the reinforcement is imbedded into the framing structure to prevent the glass from popping out of place when it is being moved. All reinforcement work can be made to appear invisible or to cross the glass in a simple pattern (see Chapter 2, design 71).

3-3. *Diamond Lights* showing the weaving type pattern that distributes the weight properly.

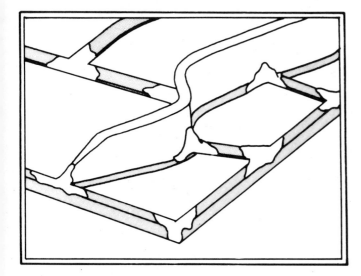

3-4. Steel reinforcement bar with one end cut to a sharp angle, soldered along the leaded joints.

Lead Came

Examine old, unrestored windows to see where buckling occurs—around name plates or other enclosed areas and along overly extended, unbroken, unreinforced lead lines.

To help distribute weight evenly, the cames should be made to interrupt each other in a weaving pattern. This effect is most obvious in the diamond pattern (fig. 3-3). If the design is not overly large, the right leading sequence plus the use of steel-core or hollow-heart lead came (with the internal steel bar in place) may provide adequate structural strength. Steel-core and hollow-heart leads may be used along straight lines that run from perimeter edge to perimeter edge. These leads cannot be bent to follow a curve too easily but can be strong enough to cope with a moderate amount of weight.

For a large design or one that is without straight lines, thin steel bars are used. They are available in various dimensions and can be purchased in different lengths. These bars can be bent in a vise to follow a curving lead line that travels from perimeter edge to perimeter edge and then soldered along that line at the leading joints (fig. 3-4). Both ends of the steel bar can be cut at an angle where they connect with the perimeters so as to minimize interference with installation.

Considering gravity's constant pull, work out your reinforcement plan well in advance of cutting glass for any design. Decide what type of reinforcement to use, the direction and lines to be reinforced, and how many lines will need this work. Distribute reinforcement bars evenly throughout a design.

Circles present special problems. Some designs call for circles or ovals to "kiss" other leads. This means that the lead around the circle touches another lead without being cut at the point of contact. At these points the leads are simply soldered together. To do this, place the cut circle inside a piece of lead came and carefully roll them both along the work surface, wrapping the lead tightly around the glass as you go. Cut the lead where the edges meet, making sure that the two ends meet securely before soldering them together. Then, lay the wrapped circle into place in the design and solder the joints where the circle lead touches other leads (fig. 3-5).

3-5. A circle being wrapped in lead came, a detail of how circles overlap or "kiss" each other, and a cut-away detail of the leads overlapping.

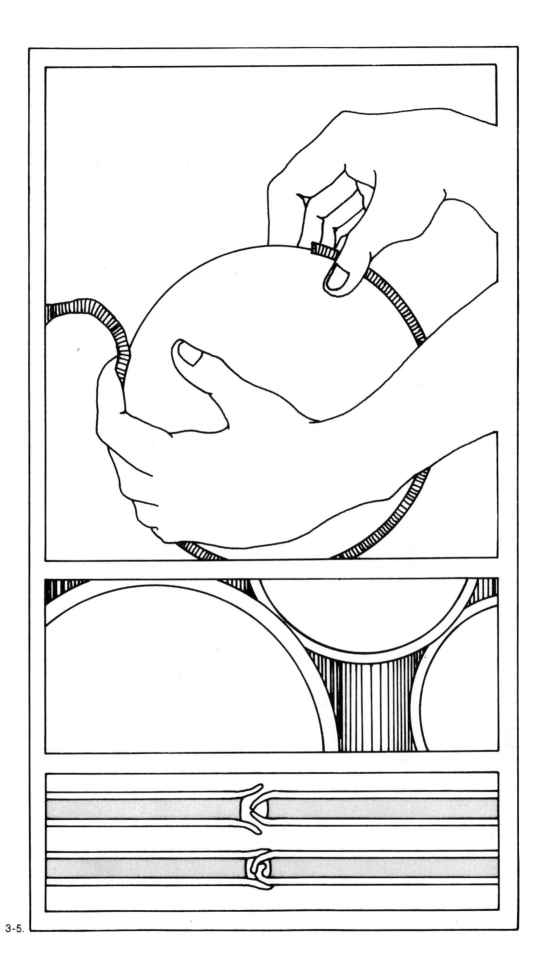

When a design is completed, with the top lead laid on, and the final lath strip nailed in position, there are a few things you can do to greatly improve your work. They are always done just before soldering the joints, and involve straightening lines, jostling leads, correcting corners, and tapping joints flat. These jobs are done somewhat simultaneously, working from one to the other.

Starting near the central area and working outwards, slip the blade of your stopping knife under the flange of a lead and give it a jiggle. If the glass is not properly seated, this action will shift it into position. Check and correct all parallel lines and corners with a straight edge and a square and adjust intersecting lines so that they give the illusion of unbroken continuity.

Use a small hammer to tap all of the joints flat. A magnetic tack hammer used for picture framing is perfect. When you are satisfied that all lead lines are as you want them, flux and solder the joints. Then brush the entire lead surface with a stiff wire brush to give the lead a beautiful finish. Be careful not to scratch the glass. (You may also want to wire brush the joints before soldering to remove grime or corrosion that might hinder your soldering work.)

3-6.

Copperfoil

Regardless of the inherent strength of copperfoil work, always reinforce the perimeter. These outer edges can be handled with 108 lead came U channel, brass U channel, or thin flat strips of brass or brass rods. Light- to medium-gauge brass wire can also be used for perimeters but it is best for the perimeters of free-form shapes and for interior reinforcement work. Shape the wire by hand so that it conforms to the lines in the design or to the perimeter of the design. If the wire is very flexible, it can be shaped and tacked into place in one operation (fig. 3–6). If not, the wire must be shaped first and then soldered in place. In either event, once the wire is covered with solder, it virtually disappears.

For large designs, reinforcement is handled with rods or strips of brass or even the thin steel bars described in the section on lead came work.

The structural strength of a panel before reinforcement depends upon how evenly the pattern is distributed, the widths of foil used, and the thicknesses of the glass. If a design is excessively concentrated in one area, the pieces of glass that support the greatest weight must be wrapped in a proportionally wider foil for added strength.

Spaces between pieces of glass, once filled with solder, help to strengthen the design (fig. 3–7). An extreme application of this natural occurrence, where spaces are intentionally created for solder to fill, is called floating (see Special Techniques below). These filled spaces, intended or not, will not properly support a large piece of glass wrapped in thin copperfoil. Although the lead line or area will be strong, the edge that grips the large piece of glass may not be strong enough to hold the glass in place. Even reinforcement work will not correct this situation, so always exaggerate the thickness of the copperfoil line until you are familiar with the relationship between the width of the copperfoil to the size of the piece of glass.

3-6. Lightweight wire being tacked into position along a copperfoil line.

3-7. A copperfoil panel wrapped and ready for soldering. The two details show a large space that would be filled by floating solder into the space and the usual small space that occurs naturally.

Structure: Three-dimensional Work

Most three-dimensional work should be handled with the copperfoil technique. It was, in part, developed for just that purpose. There is no one logical sequence of construction to follow. You can start at the end section of a design and work towards the center, start from the center area and work outwards, or even build components of the design separately and then join them together. The point is to experiment with new approaches and see what works best.

Soldering with a slightly cool iron is helpful. A hot iron is great for flat work but annoying in the elevated positions required for joints on three-dimensional objects. Use a 100-watt iron and plug into a rheostat or unplug your iron at frequent intervals to reduce and maintain a low heat.

Masking tape can be used to hold three-dimensional objects together while you are soldering as well as to span spaces between joints, thus making it possible to float solder between them (fig. 3–8).

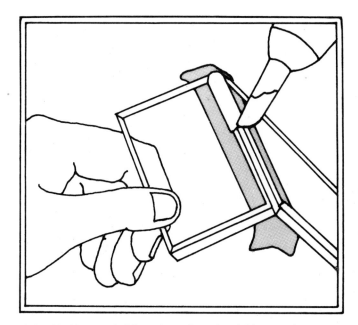

3-8.   Masking tape holding a three-dimensional object together.

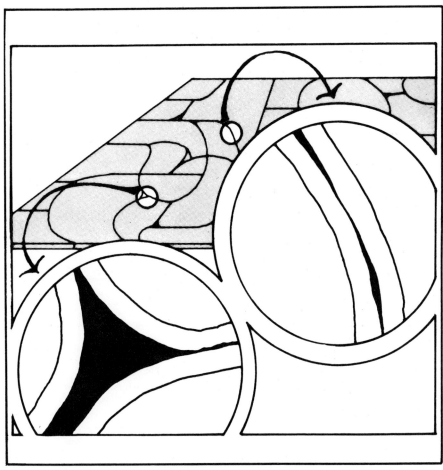

3-7

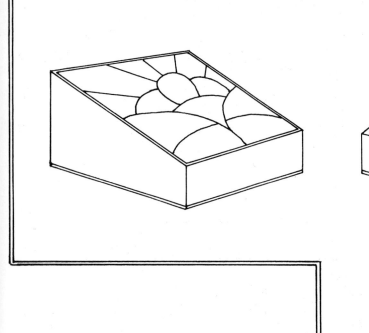

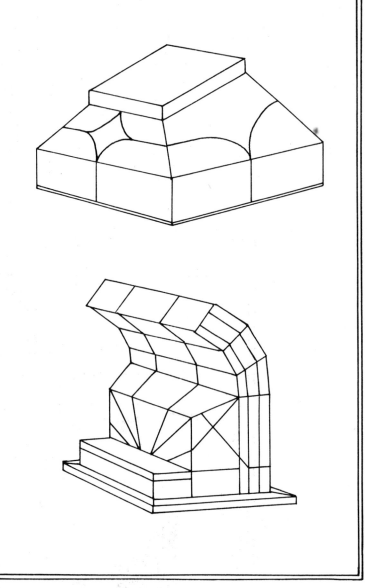

3-9.   A box with lid tilted at an angle and a box with both tilted lid and sides. The glass cash register is an example of how the idea of a simple box can be built up to be complex. (Drawing by Anthony Downes.)

Boxes

When making an enclosed object—e.g., a box—consider the glass selection carefully and decide beforehand whether the object is to be functional or decorative. If a box is to be functional, you might want to use a lot of opalescent glass that will hide its contents but still look like leaded glass. If the box is meant to be kept empty or you want its contents to show, then highly transparent, antique glass will look quite good, especially if you use mirror for the bottom to reflect light back up through the box. Never use dark antique glass for a box unless you want the glass to appear black.

If the side panels of the box are cut to a slight angle, light will be increased and the design will be more apparent. Sloping the lid gives the same effect (fig. 3–9).

The bottom section of a box is often cut after the sides have been soldered together to compensate for any small inaccuracies.

Edges that are soldered together at an angle are always important and must not be allowed to greatly overlap each other. When edges overlap, the copperfoil on one edge is often covered by the copperfoil on the other edge, making soldering difficult.

Since you want the box lid to lie flat, keep the solder as flat as possible. For added strength, solder a brass strip or U channel along the bottom perimeter of the lid and along the surface it will lie upon. Extending the lid beyond the sides of the box or adding an angled lip to the lid helps to conceal the area where the lid rests upon the box.

Lids can be hinged or removable. To make a removable lid, cut strips of brass or glass to the dimensions of the outside edge. Cut the strips at both ends to an angle of 60 degrees. Solder the strips together and then to the edge of the lid (fig. 3–10). It is a good idea to make terrarium lids completely removable so that you can control growing temperatures.

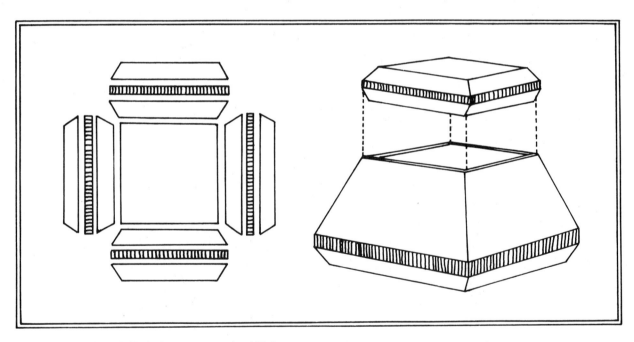

3-10.   A removable lid with the lip cut to an angle of 60 degrees.

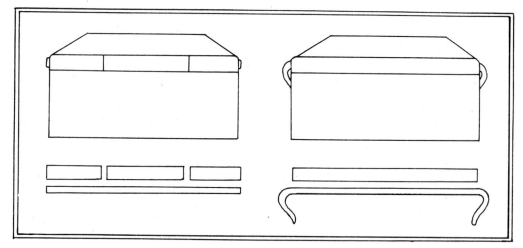

3-11A, 3-11B

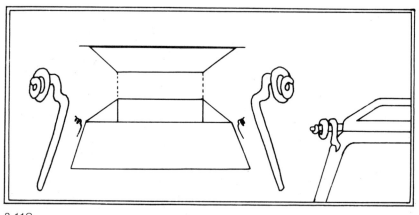

3-11C

3-12

Hinges

There are a few different ways to hinge a box, small table screen, or window section. The best methods employ a thin brass tube with an accompanying inner rod that are available from glass suppliers and model train stores.

One method is to cut the tube (but not the rod) into three sections. Solder the center section to the center of the lid and solder the two end sections of the tube to the ends of the box so that when the lid is placed on the box, the three tube sections form one continuous tube. Then slide the rod, cut to the total length of the tube, through the three sections (fig. 3–11A). The same procedure is followed for making hinges on screens except that the rod is cut slightly longer and then bent to prevent it from slipping through the tube.

The second method is to cut and solder one continuous brass tube the length of the lid or panel. A rod that is longer than the tube is then passed through the tube. The excess wire is bent at both ends and attached to the outside corners of the box or other panel. Make sure you do not bend the rod so tightly and close to the tube that it impedes opening the lid or moving the panels (fig. 3–11B).

When making tube hinges, avoid letting solder creep into the tube opening, thus sealing it closed. It is also important to cut the tube correctly. When a tube is cut, it often becomes tightly compressed, closing off the opening. If possible, use a small saw with a small section of the rod inserted so that when you saw through the tube you also saw off a bit of the rod. In this way it is easy to remove the sawed off section of rod that prevents the tube from becoming compressed.

Another way to hinge a lid is with two bent loop shapes (fig. 3–11C). Bend and solder one loop to one outside corner of the box. Then solder a rod across the lid so that it extends beyond both edges of the lid. Slip one end of the rod through the loop already soldered in place. Slip the other loop over the other end of the rod and solder the loop in position. The action is just like putting on a jacket: first one arm, then the next.

3-11. Some examples of hinging: (A) tube hinge in three sections, (B) solid tube hinge, and (C) bent loops with a rigid bar.

3-12. An extended lid resting upon the back of the box.

No matter which hinging method is used, lids will need something to keep them from flopping completely backwards when opened. This can be accomplished by soldering a chain from the inside of the lid to the interior of the box or by extending the back part of the lid so that when it is opened, it rests against the back side of the box and is stopped (fig. 3–12).

Dome Lamps

It is impossible to include an accurate pattern for a dome lamp in this book but some information may prove helpful.

Dome lamps are worked on a form. Unless the center of the form is already located for you, locate the center by laying a piece of paper under the form and tracing around the circular bottom opening. Then fold the paper in half and then in half again to locate the center of the circle. Make sure that you match up the edges of the circle when folding the paper. Place the piece of paper on the floor, beneath a table edge and locate the center point with a plumb bob. Tape the paper to the floor and mark the position for the plumb bob on the table's edge. Place the form back over the drawing, and use the plumb bob to locate the center point at the top of the form (fig. 3-13). Once you find the center of the form, use a compass to draw in the desired upper opening of the lamp that corresponds to the vase cap or other hanging apparatus you will use.

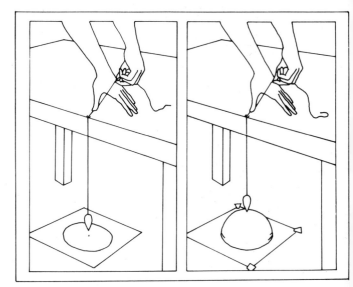

3-13. Locating the center of a dome form: how to lay out the four points, stretching a piece of string from point to point, and marking out the upper circular opening.

Draw your design directly on the form. If the form is made of wood or has already been used once before, cover it with masking tape and then draw in the design. Trace and number your pieces directly from the form. Mount the tracing paper on a stiff paper such as manila file folders and cut them out. Cut all of your glass over a light box and arrange the pieces on the box in a rough duplicate of the final design. When all of the pieces are cut, pick up one of the pieces that comprise the upper circle and check it for accuracy against the pattern on the form. Groze it for a perfect fit, wrap it in foil, and use push pins to secure it in position on the form. Pick up the next adjoining piece of the upper circle. Check the piece against the form pattern and the piece already in position. Groze for a perfect fit, wrap it in foil, and position it with nails or push pins on the form. Solder these two pieces together. (A soldering gun is very useful during the preliminary soldering stages.) Continue working in this way, removing and replacing the nails or push pins as you solder on more pieces of glass (fig. 3–14). This sequence will ensure a tight fit. Dome lamps are always worked from the top opening towards the bottom.

Use the narrowest precut foil possible or cut your own. To further decrease the width of the final lead line, wrap the glass slightly off center so that the foil edge is smaller on the front of the glass than it is on the reverse side. With opalescent glass, this discrepancy will not be visible through the glass.

To reinforce the dome, apply the finished bead to the outer surface with the lamp still on the form. Gently remove the lamp from the form and solder the inside. A slightly flat bead is used to prevent casting shadows through the glass.

After the final bead work is complete, the dome is reinforced at both circular openings and, depending upon the size of the dome, through various lines on the interior of the dome. First, heavy gauge wire is bent and soldered around the top and bottom openings (fig. 3–15). These two wire circles can either be bent by hand or professionally through a lamp shade manufacturer or other such business. All you need are the diameter measurements but for the first few times, take the shade with you.

3-14. Dome assembly showing wrapped and tacked pieces of glass supported with push pins. (Lamp by Greenbaum, see figs. C-5).

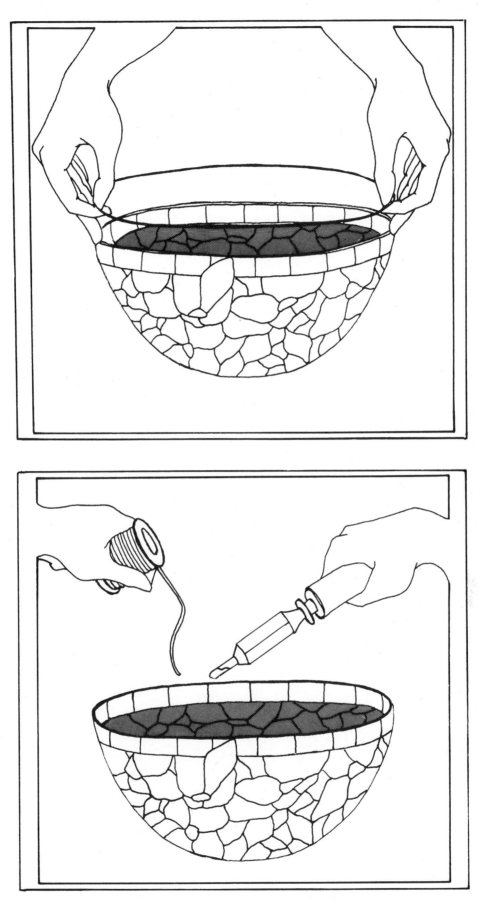

3-15.　Reinforcing the bottom circular opening.

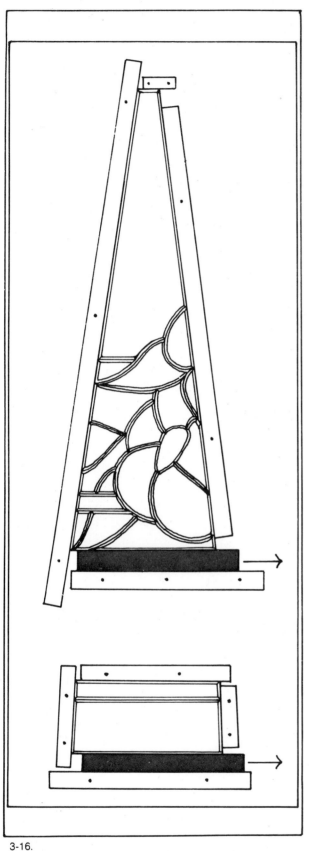

The interior is reinforced last. Select four interior lead lines that divide the lamp roughly into four parts. Starting from the wire at the top opening, solder a light-gauge wire onto these lines, bending the wire to conform to the shape of the line. Proceed downward to the bottom edge wire.

Panel Lamps

Panel lamps are easy to put together so long as the individual panels are identical in size and shape.

Before wrapping the pieces that form a single panel, lay them over a paper pattern of the design and check for accuracy; groze down any discrepancies. When you are ready to begin soldering work (thus forming the individual panel shapes), nail a lath border around a paper pattern and recheck a few of the panels in this form. Inevitably a few panels will be somewhat larger or smaller than the pattern. Adjust the lath border to fit the largest panel and spread out the pieces of glass in the smaller panels to fit within the strips of lath. When you begin to solder the panels together, the solder will fill these small spaces. Make sure to nail down the lath in such a way as to permit easy removal of each panel after it is soldered (fig. 3–16).

Once all of the basic panel shapes are soldered together, use a hot iron to remove any drips of solder from the outside edges of each panel that might interfere with joining the panels together. Wash each panel in hot water and detergent.

To put the lamp together, lay the panels reverse side up and very carefully match them together. If one panel is a hair too long, allow the excess to occur at the top of the lamp. Use plenty of masking tape in a horizontal and vertical overlapping pattern to connect the panels tightly together (fig. 3–17).

Carefully turn the panels over (fig. 3–18), lift them up, and join the last two edges so that they form the lamp shape (fig. 3–19). Tape the two end panels together. At this point work proceeds as usual: First solder the outside joints (fig. 3–20), then the inside joints (fig. 3–21), after the final head is finished, the skirts are added, layer by layer (fig. 3-22).

3-16. Panel and section of a skirt surrounded with lath strips nailed to the work surface ready for soldering. The dark piece of lath is not nailed into position and can be removed to facilitate removal of the newly soldered panels.

3-17. Panel lamp taped together on the reverse side.

3-18. Lamp turned over, ready to be lifted into shape.

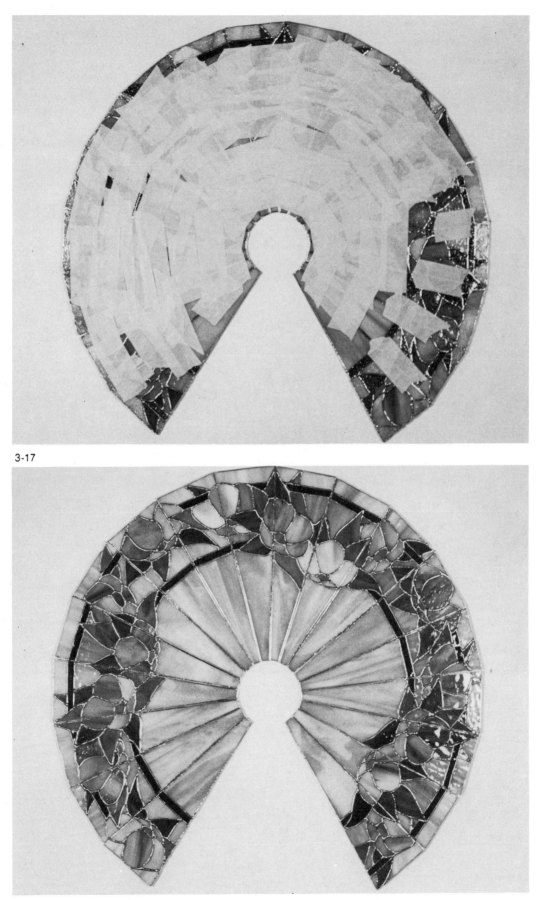

3-17

3-18

3-19

3-21

3-19.   Lamp lifted into position, ready for soldering.

3-20.   Solder being dripped down the panel joints. Final beading takes place after the panel lamp is strong enough to be moved.

3-21.   Lamp turned over with some of the tape removed. Interior joints are soldered in this position.

3-22. Finished lamp. (Lamp by French, from the Cover residence, Bronxville, New York.)

With all three-dimensional work you will encounter difficulties when soldering joints. In some instances you may be able to prop the object into position with blocks of wood but the easiest way to deal with strange angles is to work with the object held in your lap and propped against your work surface (fig. 3–23). This will leave you vulnerable to solder burns so cover your lap with a thick towel before beginning work. Also, you will find that wearing a glove on the hand that does most of the holding and moving of the object makes this type of work less painful.

For more information on designing your own panel lamps, see *Glass-Works*, published by Van Nostrand Reinhold Company.

3-23. Holding a lamp for soldering.

Special Techniques

There are many advantages to being adept at both copperfoil and lead came techniques. Don't fall into the trap of preferring one, to the total exclusion of the other. Otherwise, you will find yourself using copperfoil for a large window that would be more quickly executed in lead came or using lead came to put together a lamp better suited for copperfoil.

Along with the obvious benefits of being versatile in both techniques, there are many interesting ways to combine them in the same work to produce the best possible effect. Greenbaum's *Flight* (Chapter 2, design 23) is a good example. By using thin (86) lead came for straight lines and copperfoil for the curving lines, the contrast between rigid and flowing lines is enhanced. If the panel were to be fabricated only in lead came, the nuance of the curves would not be apparent. In the same way, to use only copperfoil would be time-consuming and the straight lines would lose some of their sharpness, especially at the corners.

Other methods for changing the look of the leaded line or for adding texture to the lead or glass can be used as embellishments to good design.

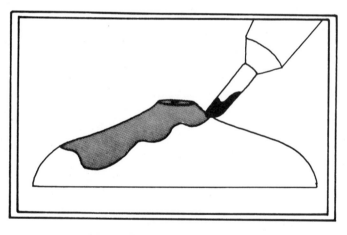

3-24.   Tinning a vase cap.

Tinning and Floating

To tin metal is to coat it with a thin layer of solder. It is done with a lot of flux, a small amount of solder, and a very hot iron. You might want to tin a decorative piece of metal to be used in a design or the vase cap on a lamp (fig. 3–24) so that it blends in with the other lead lines.

Floating is similar to tinning except that greater quantities of solder are used. Empty spaces intentionally left between pieces of glass can be floated (filled) with solder, and solder can be floated between circles placed close to each other (see Chapter 2, design 11).

Since the heat from a large concentration of molten solder in one area can cause glass to crack, work slowly and allow the glass and solder to cool periodically.

Floating can also be used to give texture to lead came by covering the lead with a rough coat of solder. Use a fairly cool iron when doing this because lead came melts rather easily.

To vary the shape of a copperfoil line so that it changes in width from slender to wide, vary the width of space between two pieces of glass; then float solder into the space. Solder can be floated over a gap between pieces of glass on a three-dimensional object by first taping the gap with masking tape to form a bridge between the two pieces of glass. A piece of cardboard can be pressed securely in place beneath a small gap so that solder can be floated to fill the area. It is especially important on three-dimensional work to work with a cool iron.

Copperfoil Overlay

This is actually a special type of floating technique. Sheet copperfoil can be cut into intricate patterns such as the veining on butterfly wings or leaves, wrapped around the glass edge, and then solder floated over the pattern (fig. 3–25). This technique can be used to imitate the metal filigree that Tiffany used on the wings of his dragonfly lamps.

The foil is cut with a sharp mat knife. The weight of the solder, once floated over the foil, will keep the pattern flat to the glass surface. For an extra delicate and extended overlay, a few tiny drops of clear epoxy will hold the pattern flat.

3-25.   Cutting sheet foil, wrapping it around a piece of glass, and floating solder over the foil.

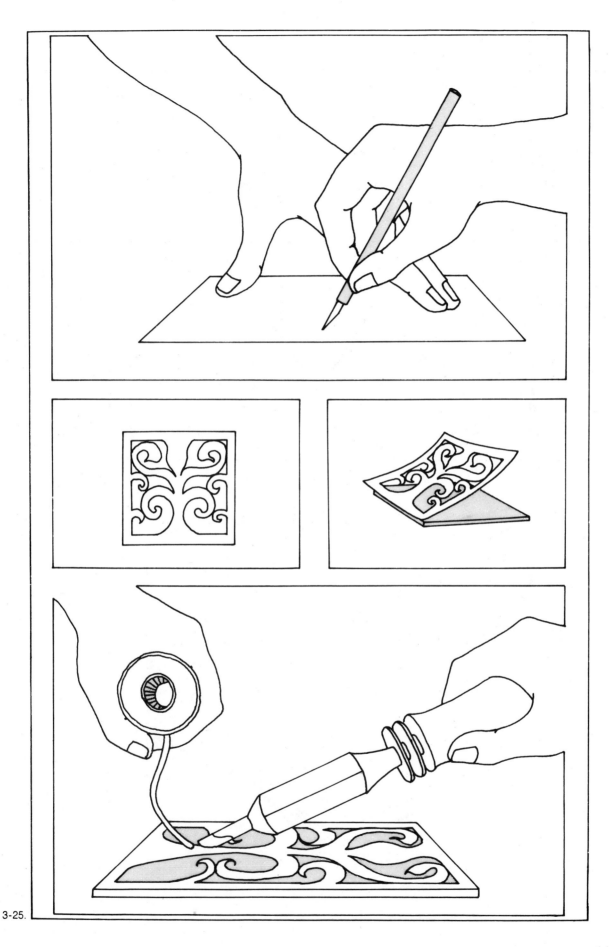

Lead Came Overlay

Sheet lead can be cut into simple or complex shapes, held in place with epoxy, or silicone, and then soldered to an existing lead line (see chapter 2, design 9). Floating solder over the joint between the lead line and the piece of sheet lead will make them appear to be one continuous shape. Any roughness at the joint can be sanded smooth. At a distance, it will look as if the glass, rather than the lead, was cut to a strange and exotic shape (fig. 3–26).

Carving Lead Came

Instead of using different widths of lead in the same design to add visual variety, you can make a single line expand and contract in one graceful sweep by actually carving the lead itself. First, build up the width of the flange by cutting sheet lead into strips and attaching them by floating solder over the joining line. The flange can be increased to a two-inch width or greater. Then, cut the flange away with a mat knife to the desired width and shape (fig. 3-27).

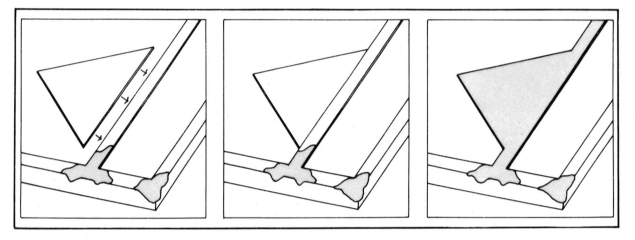

3-26. Sheet lead, cut and being attached to a lead line.

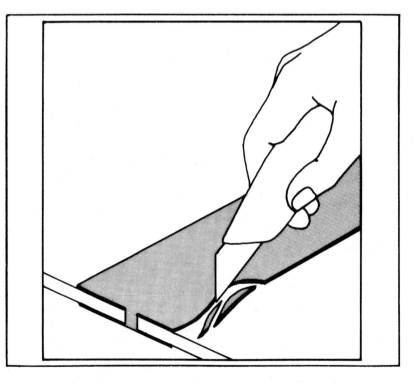

3-27. Cutting away the flange with a matte knife.

Do not attempt to do this until the lead and glass are in place and be careful not to cut away so much of the flange as to expose the heart.

Plating Glass

This is a wonderful technique but it ages poorly. Plating is the method of joining two pieces of glass (or other materials) so that they act as one. The reason for the cautionary note is that over a period of time moisture can condense between the two pieces of glass and discolor the whole area. Tiffany used this technique often. To restore his plated work today, the plated pieces of glass must be separated and all sorts of accumulated grime cleaned away.

Despite the difficulties, there are many interesting effects that can be created with this technique. It can be used to create a new color, to imitate the effect of a hazy mist over a scene, or to add texture to another piece of glass. The possibilities are numerous. To give a mirror-like sheen to light-colored antique glass, the glass can be plated to mirror or a piece of highly polished tin. Objects, such as Chinese paper cuts, wild flowers, photographs, etc. can be sandwiched between two pieces of glass. One difficulty with this technique is the tendency of flux to creep between the two plating materials while you are working. You must either use flux super-sparingly or a dry flux called Styrene, which is made in a candle form available through plumbing supply stores.

There are two different methods for plating with lead came. Two pieces of glass can be leaded together at the same time in one U channel or each piece can be leaded separately and then soldered together to form one unit (fig. 3–28). In the first instance, use two pieces of glass that are thin enough to fit together between the flange of a regular lead or use a double- or wide-heart lead. Cut the two pieces identically, clean them well, and tape them together at the edges with scotch tape. The tape edges that show beyond the flange are cut off after the entire design has been leaded. Meanwhile the tape helps prevent cement and flux from creeping between the two layers of glass plus keeps the two pieces of glass from shifting around. With the second method, plating takes place after the design has been completely leaded, cemented, and cleaned. Wrap the piece of glass that will be plated onto the finished design in U channel. Place the piece in position and solder it along the outside edges that touch the piece below.

3-28. *Top*, cut away details of the two methods for plating glass with lead came and *bottom*, details of the two methods of plating with copperfoil.

Both methods used for plating lead came work can be used for copperfoil work, with one exception (fig. 3–28). When you put the final bead on the design, leave the area flat around the pieces that will be plated. When the design is clean and thoroughly dry, wrap and solder the pieces to be plated into position. The second layer should be just a bit smaller than the piece to which it is being plated to allow for a secure bond. Use a small amount of flux and float solder along the edges that are in contact with the piece below. Clean the area with a damp cloth or whiting powder and antique with care.

When you plate tin to glass, the effect is not exactly like that of mirror but does reflect a similar polish. In this case, cut the tin to the exact dimension of the piece of glass, wrap both tin and glass together as one piece, and solder to the design.

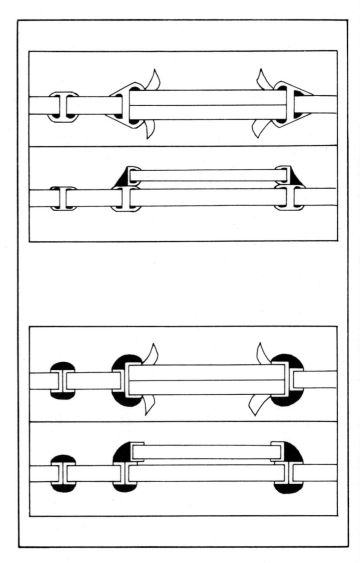

Mirror

Mirror can be used for bottoms of boxes, on the outside lower part of terrariums to hide the soil, and for hand and wall mirrors to name a few ideas. It should be cut with a steel wheel rather than a carbide cutter on the reflective, mirror side. The silver backing is rather fragile and should always be protected from scratches. One solution is to cut all of the mirror for a design and then spray the silvered side with epoxy paint.

During the soldering stage, be careful not to touch the hot iron to the epoxy and if some small beads of solder stick to the paint, leave them alone. The epoxy is not a miracle protector but just a good safeguard. To further protect the silvered side on boxes and hand mirrors that will be moved around, cover the epoxy with felt contact paper once you have finished soldering. If you ever have to remove the felt contact paper, the epoxy should prevent the silver from being lifted off.

Additional Craft Tips

The following list is of miscellany that should prove to be helpful.

1. Use a steel wheel cutter for antique, semiantique, mirror, and window glass. Use a carbide cutter for opalescent, plate, and thickly textured, industrial glass. Use a small wheel for curves and a large wheel for straight lines. (Actually, all cutters are interchangeable but using different cutters for different glass makes work that much easier.)

2. For accurate cuts, practice scoring as slowly as possible.

3. In repeat patterns cut all of the pieces that are the same color and size at the same time. For production work involving geometric shapes, you may want to purchase one of the moderately priced cutting machines. These machines can help you cut a hundred pieces of glass in about an hour. Also, two other new tools worth investigation are a diamond band saw and the new electric grozing machines. These tools are advertised in the three leading glass magazines: *Studio, Glass,* and *Stained Glass.*

4. Use cut running pliers for thick glass and curves and a circle cutter for perfect circles.

5. When cutting a deep curve, first score the desired line; then score the smaller internal lines, rather than the reverse. To remove a circle from the center of a sheet of glass without drilling or blasting the hole, score the circular area to be removed, and tap it with your knuckle. Then score a few concentric circles within this area, with each new circle heading nearer the center. The area within the center circle is then scored over and over again with crisscrossed lines. All of the other circles are then scored (fig. 3–29). The circles are tapped out in sequence starting from the center area.

6. Whenever a cutter does not work well, it is damaged, dull, or you are using too much or too little pressure in cutting.

7. Use adhesive tape on the backside of all straight edges to prevent them from slipping on the glass surface. For very long cuts, use heavy-weight, double-sided tape on the backside of the straight edge so that it sticks to the glass during scoring.

8. If a copperfoil line is slightly rough, smooth it with fine grit sandpaper or fine steel/brass wool; otherwise, rework the line. Rough joints on lead came work can also be sanded smooth. Always be very careful when sanding because glass scratches very easily.

9. For soldering copperfoil use water-soluble flux or zinc chloride. For lead came use Styrene candles or oleic acid.

10. A soldering gun is very useful for tacking glass together.

11. Use liquid detergent to clean flux and grit from copperfoil; liquid Joy detergent works best. For removing flux when you use oleic acid or when cleaning plated glass, use whiting powder or plaster of paris.

12. To protect your hands while soldering, wear thin cotton gloves or use one of the special creams, such as Kerodex 71, made for coating your hands with a protective covering. Another idea is to lather your hands with bar soap, then rub your hands together until the suds disappear and wave them around until they dry. Also, scratch dry soap under your nails. Always wear rubber gloves when you antique solder.

13. Copperfoil can be antiqued a copper bronze color with cupric nitrate or sulfate. Buy it in powder form and mix it yourself to make a saturated solution. Although cupric sulfate is available in most glass supply stores in a liquid form, it is still a lot cheaper to mix your own.

14. Before applying antiquing solution, first clean the solder but do not let it dry. The extra water will help the antiquing solution to get into hidden areas. Apply the solution and wipe any excess off the glass but avoid rubbing the solder lines until later. Always allow the solution to sit for a few hours and then clean the glass with whiting powder or plaster of paris to give the lead a good finish and to polish the glass. If a finished work has been allowed to sit around awhile without being antiqued, clean the lines with steel/brass wool and then apply the solution.

15. To waterproof a terrarium, lay a thick line of silicone glue over the inner lead lines so that the glue covers the area where the lead touches the glass.

16. Reproducing effects on glass photographically is a recent development. Coat a sheet of glass with Rockland Print E-Mulsion (available from Rockland Colloid Corp., 302 Piermont Avenue, Piermont, New York, 10968). The glass can then be exposed and put through the processing baths as if it were photographic paper.

17. One additional note of caution concerns the question of lead poisoning, which has been debated for some

time without a conclusive decision. Assume the worst and never eat or drink while soldering; keep your hands away from your mouth until they are thoroughly cleaned; place a fan in your window so that it draws the fumes away from you; and try to avoid inhaling fumes. Unless you find it uncomfortable, wear light-weight cotton gloves while soldering. Goggles worn through all stages of work are also a good suggestion.

18. If you want more information on the hazards of working with stained glass and other crafts, write to Art Hazards Project, Center for Occupational Hazards Inc., 56 Pine Street, New York, New York, 10005.

19. If you plan to use acid etching techniques, also plan on wearing a full rubber outfit and constructing a truly elaborate ventilation system. The acid is highly poisonous.

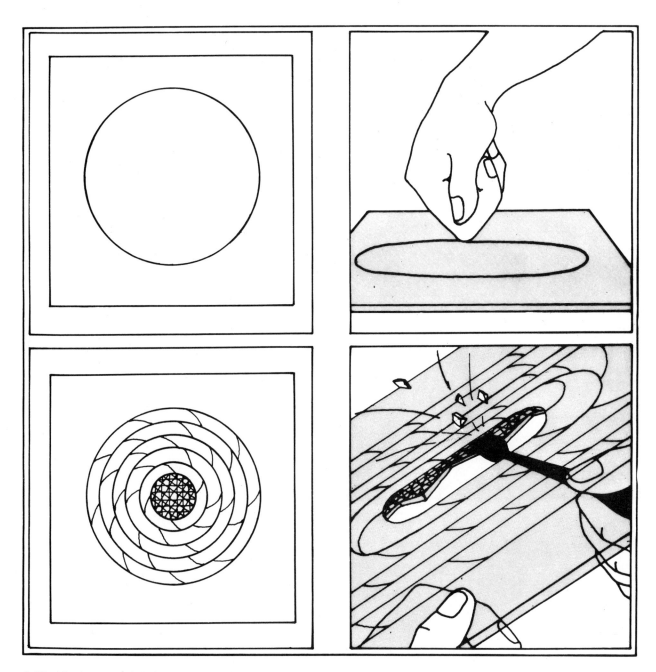

3-29.   Cutting out a circle from the sheet of glass.

4.

PHOTOGRAPHY

The following information on photographing stained glass is offered to help you keep accurate records of your work, to have slides to submit for publications and exhibitions, and to make a presentation book that can be shown to prospective clients.

The material is divided into several sections and unless you are already familiar with such terms as direct positive printing, depth of field, bounce lighting, etc., it is advisable to read each section thoroughly since these terms are not explained each time they appear. Also if you are just embarking on photography, it will be very helpful to refer to your camera and light meter instruction booklets as you read the following material. Another suggestion is to skip the section on Setting Up Shots, read the rest of the chapter, and then return to that section.

The camera is basically a simple tool that is even called "the idiot box" by some old pros (not to be confused with the other idiot box that is usually found plugged into the wall). The information gained by photographing your glass is applicable to all photography, and a successful shooting can generate enough excitement to carry you onto other facets of the craft.

On the strength that the camera gives us a print, it is a wonderful tool. In comparison to the original camera, our eyes, it is a clumsy and mediocre imitation. It is just as easy to be overwhelmed by the dials, doodads, and lingo of the camera as it is to be by the world of stained glass. It is also worth about as much—nothing. Photography may not be overly difficult, but it is limited. For instance, it is nearly impossible to exactly duplicate the interplay between glass and light on film. A panel mounted in a window in your living room, lighted by daylight and shot without correcting the interior light will produce a picture of a black room and an overly brilliant panel. Colors tend to shift all over the place, and

lamps have hot (too bright) spots with dull shadowy areas while they float in a sea of blackness. Until you get a real understanding of the problems, glass photography seems a mean business indeed. You should also be forewarned that regardless of your expertise with glass photography, the "real McCoy" will always look better. The object then is to get as close to reality as possible and to develop your sense of compromise in the process.

To shoot glass, you must understand the three lighting conditions—daylight, tungsten, and fluorescent light—and how these conditions affect glass, film, and the surrounding environment. Fortunately, if you understand the solution for one shooting, then all other similar shootings are that much easier to understand.

Setting Up Shots

The first step in setting up a stained glass shooting is to size up the situation and your needs correctly. Once you have analyzed the problems, gather together all the equipment, props, materials, and extra hands needed to get the job done. Always avoid just picking up a camera and trying to get the picture in a hit-or-miss fashion because you'll almost always miss.

There are a few general points common to all glass photography. Always take a reflected light reading with your light meter held (in the camera or your hand) within a few inches of the glass surface. If there are areas of clear or light-colored glass and areas of dark glass within the same design, take a reading from both extreme areas and average them out for the ideal reading. Always set your F/stop first and then adjust the shutter speed setting, never the reverse. Film is the cheapest commodity in photography, with your time being the most valuable, so never spare the film to get the shot. Always bracket your shots by at least 1/2 stops and preferably by

1/3 stops. Never point a light directly at glass because it will cause glare.

There is a natural tendency to take overly tight shots, to shoot the glass in the way that you want to see it in the final picture. Always allow yourself an ample border around everything that you shoot and then crop out what you do not want in the final print. With slides black tape can be used to cover an excessive border; otherwise, you will have a very small margin for error—incorrect slide mounting, the image being too close to the border of the negative, etc.

Experiment with shooting the glass from different views, bracketing each view before you move to a new position. For example, a distance shot shows how the glass looks in its environment and gives architectural scale to the work; a moderate close-up (with border) gives a clear view of the glass as a whole; and an ultra close-up shows craft work and other important details. All three views are necessary to accurately describe your work. Variants on these basic views are also very helpful. Photography is part and parcel the world of illusion, and you'll sometimes find that a new and novel view best conveys the emotional content of your work while in truth distorting reality. The Cubist painters proved that you don't just see a table head-on, but actually perceive it through a thousand different glimpses of the table. By moving away from what is thought to be realistic, you may capture a better sensation of reality.

Avoid extreme F/stop openings, i.e., if the maximum and minimum openings of your lens are F/1.4 and F/16 respectively, then shoot at one stop away from these openings. Camera lenses do not generally work at their best when taken to the limits of their capabilities. They distort.

The following vignettes are situations that I have encountered and my own trial-and-error solutions. They are not the only approaches possible, and you should take what they have to offer and improve on them.

If you are new at photography, the best recommendation is to read as much as you can tolerate. There are at least a dozen good general publications on the subject. They are all full of sound technical information, and photography is a technical art form.

Tungsten Lighted Objects
Moderate and Ultra Close-up Shots

Whether the object is a lamp or sculpture and is hung, mounted on a wall, or free standing, the situation is essentially the same. The glass should be isolated against a neutral backdrop and all but tungsten lights should be turned off or shut out. The object will need to be lighted from within and without by 3200° K bulbs. Also plan on having a tripod, cable release, light stands, reflectors, a roll of aluminum foil or white bristol board cards, and some gaffer's tape. Use either Kodak Ektachrome 50 or 160 film, 20 or 36 exposures. For a moderate close-up use a normal or macro lens. For an ultra close-up use a normal lens with an extension ring or a macro lens.

Place the object in front of the neutral backdrop or have two people hold the backdrop behind the object or rig up a clothesline to hold the backdrop. Set up the camera and tripod and begin experimenting with bounce lighting. When everything seems right, remove the camera from the tripod, take a meter reading with all the lights on, replace the camera on the tripod, and bracket your shots (fig. 4–1).

Distance Shots

Shoot the object in its natural surroundings but remove anything in the immediate area that seems too distracting. Close off or shut out any conflicting light source, and light the object with 3200°K bulbs. Bounce light off the ceiling and replace the house bulb in any lamp that will be included in the photograph with a 3200° K bulb. Use either Kodak Ektachrome 50 or 160 film in 20- or 36-exposure rolls. The lens to use is either a normal or wide angle lens.

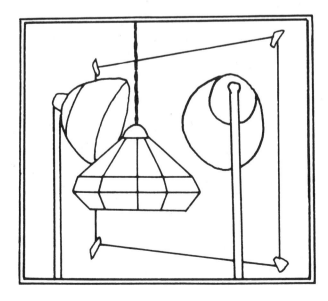

4-1. Lighting arrangement for shooting tungsten-lighted objects.

Interior Windows

If you want to shoot glass that is part of a wall or door which leads into another room, you will encounter a number of problems. The primary problem is how much of the view beyond the glass you want to have in sharp focus and how to handle the lighting behind the glass. First, close off and shut out any conflicting light source, replace all house bulbs in lamps that will be seen through the glass with 3200°K bulbs, and bounce a light off the ceiling in the room where you set up your camera and tripod. Use the same films as recommended above.

Turn on all of the lights and with a normal lens on your camera, depress the preview button, and check how the scene appears at each F/stop. If you are not pleased with any of the effects, change lenses. A long lens, around the 150–200mm range may give you good results when set at a wide aperture of F/3.5 or more, but check each opening while depressing the preview button. If you find a setting that seems correct but the light is lacking, then add bounce lighting behind the glass. Be careful to place the light stands out of camera range. If after you have tried a few experiments and none of the results are satisfactory, then set up neutral backdrops behind the glass and try it that way. The photograph will be fairly dull looking, but at least you will have a record of your work.

Daylighted Exterior Windows
Moderate and Ultra Close-up Shots

Use Kodak Ektachrome 64 or 200 film in rolls of 20 or 36 exposures. You may or may not need a tripod and extra (blue flood) lights, but it would be advisable to have them on hand. If the window has been installed high up off the ground, then a ladder would prove helpful. Also reflective white cards, aluminum foil, and a friend for assistance could make the difference in a successful shooting.

Use a macro or normal lens for moderate close-up shots and a macro or normal lens with an extension ring for ultra close-up shots.

First ascertain how much of the view beyond the glass you want to have in sharp focus. It is generally a good idea to have the background blurred; therefore, a wide aperture opening, such as F/2, may prove the best selection. The way to check for the correct opening is to depress the preview button and study the scene while changing the F/stops. To raise the light level outside the window, have a friend hold aluminum foil or white cards so that they reflect natural light into the dark areas. It is also possible to mount foil or cards onto light stands and place them outside the window, but a friend or a combination of the two is often easier to move around.

Always study and shoot glass lighted by daylight at different times of the day and under different lighting conditions since each change will affect the way that the glass looks.

Distance Shots

All of the above information applies to the following. A distance shot will include a portion of the room, and you will have to change the interior lighting so that it will be correct for daylight film. Replace all house bulbs in lamps that will be seen in the picture with blue flood lights. Also bounce blue floods off of the ceiling to raise the general light level of the room. You may want to run a few different experiments with extra lights to achieve a natural-looking balance between the glass and interior lighting. When the eye perceives the room's light as being too bright, the balance is probably correct for film.

Miscellaneous Situations
Fluorescent Lighting

Fluorescent and daylight are close to each other in color temperature; therefore, you should not be overly upset if some daylighted areas will be visible in the final photograph. Always use the correct filter combination for the specific type of fluorescent bulb (see Films). Also always shoot glass lighted by fluorescent bulbs at a shutter speed setting of at least 1/60th of a second or more; otherwise, the moving particles within the fluorescent tubes and your shutter speed will not be synchronized and black spaces will be apparent in the photograph.

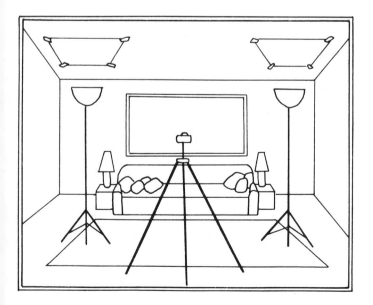

4-2. Lighting arrangement for shooting glass lighted by daylight at a distance.

Erecting a Stage

A box, terrarium, or sculpture not lighted internally can be photographed under either tungsten or daylight conditions, but in order to light it properly, you may want to build a stage. A stage allows light to be reflected up through the bottom of the object. It consists of two sturdy supports, placed approximately two and one-half to three feet (.75—.9m) apart, with a sheet of plate glass or thick acrylic plastic rested between them.

To shoot in tungsten light, position the stage near a wall and tape a neutral-colored bed sheet or a large, semitransparent sheet of paper to the wall so that it drapes behind and beneath the object placed on the stage (fig. 4–3). Then place one light beneath the stage, and bounce light off of the back of the neutral backdrop. You may want to soften this light by using reflective white cards or aluminum foil. Use a small F/stop for the greatest depth of field. This type of shooting takes a bit of fooling with to get correctly, but it is worth the effort.

To shoot in daylight, set the stage outdoors, place some crumpled aluminum foil beneath the stage to reflect light, and set the object on the stage. To throw the background completely out of focus and thus eliminate the need for a neutral backdrop, shoot with a long lens in the 150–200mm range and use a wide-open F/stop. Try to arrange your shooting on a partially overcast day for optimum lighting.

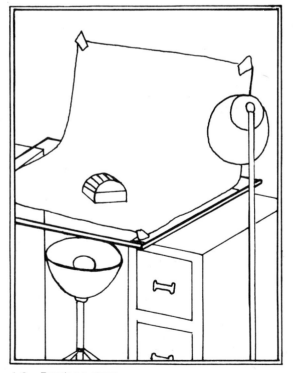

4-3. Erecting a stage.

Mirrors

Always shoot mirrors under two different circumstances, with the mirror reflecting the room's interior and with the mirror reflecting nothing. When shooting a reflected image, it is advisable to depress the preview button and change F/stops until the right amount of blurring occurs. To make the mirror reflect nothingness, have a friend hold up a sheet of paper so that it blocks out any reflection. For a sharp image always focus on the leadlines of the mirror and not on the mirror's surface.

Difficult Installations

Windows that are mounted high overhead and cannot be brought to eye level (center of subject) with the help of a ladder should be shot with a PC lens (persepctive-correction) or a view camera equipped with tilts and swings to correct linear distortion; otherwise, your glass will appear to be angled towards a point at the top of the window.

If you want to shoot a very large mural or there is not enough space for you to step back and get the entire work into one shot, use a wide- or ultra-wide-angle lens. Most of the new lenses in this category are nearly distortion free except at the edges. If you allow a large border around the mural, then all or most of the distortions will occur in empty, unimportant space that can be cropped out.

In summary, if you are new at photography, the shot is really important, and your time is limited, then hire a professional photographer who is knowledgeable with stained glass. Make sure that you are present for the shooting, and you will have double your money's worth: you will have learned how to handle the particular shooting and saved yourself a great deal of ulcer-inducing aggravation.

Equipment

Photographers are notorious gadget hounds, and with this in mind the recommended equipment has been kept to a minimum. If you decide to experiment with more complex equipment and solutions such as strobes, light slaves, artificially created backgrounds, etc., this information will still prove valuable, if only as a starting point.

Camera

The 35mm SLR (single lens reflex) camera is a simple-to-use, highly portable, and relatively inexpensive professional tool. Larger format cameras that produce 2 1/4″ square (5.72cm sq.) or 4″ × 5″ (10.16cm × 12.7cm), etc. negatives will give you better quality but the increased cost of these cameras may not justify the gain. Kodak has so much faith in the quality of 35mm film that they often blow up a shot to fill the 16′ × 60′ (4.8m × 18m) advertising space in Grand Central Station in New York City. If it's good enough for the Great Yellow Father....

Meters

A through-the-lens metering system is perfect for stained glass photography, especially when you are using zoom and medium- to long-range lenses. If your camera is not so equipped, then a hand-held meter will do just fine. Moreover, a hand-held meter explains the metering of light in a way that could never be understood through any other type of system.

When you take a meter reading with a hand-held meter, you are given a set of alternative F/stops (lens or aperture openings) and shutter-speed settings. For instance, you might get a spread of choices that looks like this: F/16 at 1/15th of a second, F/11 at 1/30th, F/8 at 1/60th, F/5.6 at 1/125th, F/4 at 1/250th, and so on (fig. 4–4). You must then choose the combination that best suits the situation. For example, to stop the action of a car race, you would choose at least F/4 at 1/250th because a 250th of a second is probably fast enough to freeze fast motion. To pick up the details of a busy street scene, you would choose F/8 at 1/60th because a 60th of a second is fast enough to freeze the medium speeds involved with milling crowds while F/8 gives you a large depth of field (area in sharp focus, ex-

4-4. Meter reading spread showing possible shutter speeds and aperture openings.

plained later). If you wanted to photograph a flower in crisp detail, you would then steady the flower, mount the camera on a tripod, and shoot at F/16 and 1/15th. This selection would give you the largest depth of field, but since the slow speed of a 15th of a second would make the camera unstable, the camera and the flower would have to be made steady. Explanations on how to make these types of decisions follow, but suffice it to say that each time you take a photograph, these decisions must be made. Understanding your camera's F/stops in relation to shutter speeds and being able to previsualize your results is prelude to controlling the camera. The manipulation of these two factors is also what determines the visual impact of your photographs.

When you're working with a through-the-lens metering system or an electric camera, the same group of combinations mentioned above are available to you except that they are happening somewhat invisibly, i.e., with a through-the-lens system, you change the F/stop (or shutter-speed setting), and the metering needle swings off the center mark until you adjust the speed (or F/stop) and bring the needle back to center. With an electric camera you change the F/stop and the speed changes automatically (or vice versa). Some of the earliest models of electric cameras are not quite up to the flexibility of the newer models or even the standard manuals. If you encounter any difficulties metering stained glass or with other techniques mentioned in this chapter, it is best to take the camera and possibly some stained glass to your local camera store for their advice.

No matter what type of metering system you use, always take the light reading from within a few inches in front of the glass; otherwise, ambient light may mislead the light meter. If you cannot get close enough to the glass to take the reading correctly, then you have a few choices. With a through-the-lens system, mount a zoom lens on the camera and zoom in as close as possible for the reading, or if your hand-held meter accepts a spot-meter attachment, then attach one and take as small an angle reading as possible or beg, borrow, or rent a spot meter or guess at the settings and bracket (explained later) like crazy. If you are ever forced to use the last suggestion, don't hesitate to use twenty shots just to get one picture, that is, if the picture is important. If you are using a hand-held meter, never take an incident reading of stained glass because this will cause your shots to be too dark (consult your owner's manual). Always take a reflected light reading.

Lenses

The normal lens, which is generally somewhere around the 50mm size, is often sold with new cameras. Many professional photographers consider it an unnecessary lens because they do not use it that often. If you are about to buy a 35mm camera, you may want to follow their thinking and purchase a more versatile lens. This will most assuredly increase the cost of your equipment. If the camera store is reputable and willing to give you a guarantee on their used equipment, then purchase the camera body new and buy a used lens.

A few suggestions for lenses include a 55mm macro, a 35mm wide angle, a medium to long range zoom lens, or one of the combination lenses that incorporate a few different lenses all in one. Your needs will dictate what you purchase, but as a guide you will need a macro or close-focusing lens for close-up detail shots, a normal lens for normal shots (it's not as undefined as it sounds), a wide angle for those times that you cannot get far enough away from the glass to take a photograph, and a medium to long range zoom for those times when you cannot get close enough. If you have tons of money and an assistant to cart this stuff around, then by all means purchase one of each. If not, a normal lens can be converted into a close-focusing lens with an extension ring and into a medium to long range lens with a Tele Converter. An even better suggestion is to buy a combination lens. An example of the latter may combine a close-focusing, a normal, and a long range lens with zoom ability. There are two drawbacks to this type of lens. It is heavy and expensive. However, a tripod will justify the weight and the combination lens is still less expensive than the lenses it replaces.

Whenever you come across a situation that your stock of equipment cannot handle, more often than not you can rent a special lens to solve the specific problem. Write to the people who manufacture lenses for your make of camera and get information on their line of special lenses.

Depth of Field and Preview Button

When you focus on an object, a certain area in front of and behind the object is also in focus. This total area is called the depth of field, and it changes each time you change the F/stop on your lens. A minimum depth of field occurs when the lens is wide open (fig. 4–5); a maximum depth of field occurs when the lens is closed down (fig. 4–6). When you open up or close down a lens, it is imitative of how your eye operates; in bright sunlight the pupil becomes a pinpoint (or F/16) and in a dark room the pupil opens wide (or F/1.4). Where the eye and the camera diverge completely is that the eye attempts

to maintain the maxium depth of field in any lighting situation whereas the camera lens fluctuates dramatically depending upon where you set the F/stop. This apparent disadvantage, when planned for, is a great benefit to the photographer and actually enhances reality. If you are photographing a window behind which is a busy street scene, opening up the lens all the way will blur the activity behind the window into formless areas of light and dark. On the other hand, shooting a lamp with the lens wide open will produce a photograph of the lamp partially in and partially out of focus.

There are three exercises for understanding depth of field. Check each lens that you own, and most probably you will discover vertical lines beneath the focusing ring. These lines are often color

4-5. Minimum depth of field.

4-6. Maximum depth of field.

coded to the F/stops, and they indicate the area that will be in focus when the lens is set to a specific F/stop (fig. 4–7). The measurements will be indicated in both feet and meters. Learn to use these as a way of checking your area of sharp focus. The second exercise is to set up a few tests and then examine the results. Use the two examples mentioned above (shooting a window and a lamp), mount the camera on a tripod or another stationary object, and shoot the glass at every F/stop on the aperture ring. Adjust the speeds accordingly. The third exercise is to visually select the desired depth of field by either using the preview button on your camera or if you have preset lenses, by changing the F/stops while the diaphragm of the lens is closed down. Depressing the preview button or closing down the diaphragm allows you to preview the picture before you take it. It is best to have the camera mounted on a tripod when you use this technique so that you can then remove the camera, take it up to the glass for a meter reading (set only the shutter speed and leave the F/stop where it is), and then return the camera to the tripod and take the shot. The tripod insures that you will return to the exact position from which you made your F/stop selection. As a general rule, three-dimensional objects should be shot at a small F/stop (i.e., F/16) and flat surfaces can be shot at either a small or large F/stop.

4-7. Vertical depth of field markings on a lens.

Tripod

One rather misleading conception about owning a 35mm camera is that you can shoot anything under any condition. You become accustomed to shooting on the run and without extra lights or a tripod. In spite of its impressive portability and the superfast films that can be pushed (explained under Films) to make them even faster, the 35mm is a limited tool. If you want professional-looking shots, then you must approach the subject with some professionalism.

A tripod allows you a total range of F/stops, frees your hands and person for holding extra lights or making adjustments to the scene, and generally makes life easier. As a rule of thumb, any shutter speed below 1/30th of a second on a 35mm SLR can only be used when the camera is mounted on a secure base; otherwise, the chance of blurred pictures is excellent. What do you do when the sun is setting and it's the last chance that you will have to get a shot of your best window before it's flown to Alaska, and you don't own a tripod? The answer is to either have blurry photographs, shots of the glass artificially lighted, or very dark photographs. Consider the tripod an investment and purchase one of the better brands such as a Tiltall or another brand similar in weight and portability. A good solid tripod is the only safe support for your expensive camera equipment.

Cable Release

Once you have your tripod, the problems of camera shake are not completely solved. Below 1/30th of a second you should not use your finger to trigger the shutter. Either buy a cable release or use the self-timer on your camera, if it is so equipped.

Lighting

A collection of clamp lights, lightweight light stands, and reflectors of the 12″ (30.48cm) Smith-Victor type, plus a few other and sundry gadgets are vital to photographing almost everything, especially artificially lighted glass. These lighting outfits are simple to use since you place the light where your eye sees that it is needed. Their cost is nominal. Later you can purchase all kinds of sophisticated lighting equipment but for starters buy at least three sets of clamps, stands, and reflectors.

Color film is balanced for specific types of light and in order to get the most out of film, it is important to try to meet ideal lighting conditions. Tungsten color film is sold for indoor shooting but is actually not balanced for indoor house bulbs. Tungsten film is balanced for 3200° Kelvin bulbs, available in your camera store and made to be used in the above mentioned lighting units. They come in two wattages: 250 and 500. If you are shooting with tungsten film, then you must use 3200°K bulbs or else the glass will appear slightly yellowish. (Since this warming distortion is often very appealing and may convey the feeling of the glass better than the coolness of reality, you may want to experiment with both house and 3200°K bulbs.)

Daylight color film is balanced for both natural daylight (which is the approximate equivalent of between 5000°K and 5800°K) plus electronic flash, blue flash, and blue floodlights. Blue floods are used in the above described lighting units. There is no special film for shooting in fluorescent light although daylight film is the closest match. Generally you either use special color-compensating filters (see Film) with tungsten or daylight film or, in a pinch, shoot with daylight film. It will occasionally happen that you want to shoot a lamp or other glass when two or more conflicting light sources are present. The light sources must be simplified to a single source, i.e., the draperies drawn to shut out daylight, the overhead fluorescent light extinguished, and the lamp shot with 3200°K bulbs and tungsten film.

There is something wonderfully compulsive and pedantic about photography. Once you know the basic three lighting situations, the solutions are always immediately apparent. It's the rest of life that is unpredictable. (What do you mean the fluorescent lights can't be turned off?) Learning how to outthink existing circumstances and to get your shots in spite of obstacles is one of the elements of good photography.

Lighting Techniques

To properly light your work, there should be light in front of as well as behind the glass. Since lights cannot be aimed directly at the frontal glass surface without causing glare, indirect lighting techniques, called bounce lighting, must be used. Bounce lighting means bouncing light off a reflective surface—a ceiling, wall, crumpled aluminum foil, aluminum foil cardboard, or white bristol board cards—so that the softened light is reflected onto the glass.

The standard starting point for setting up lights is to place two light stands, plus reflectors and bulbs, on either side of the glass you want to photograph, midway between the glass and the camera.

4-8. Aluminum foil and a white card in position on reflectors.

Then, depending upon your needs, the reflectors are either aimed at the ceiling, wall, or neutral backdrop (see Setting Up Shots). To use the aluminum foil or white cards, the reflectors are aimed in a general upwards position and the cards or foil are attached to the rim of the reflectors so that they catch the light and bounce it back onto the glass (fig. 4-8). Another use for the cards and foil is to gather ambient light and reflect it into specific small areas.

In order to keep the light pure and untainted by any other color, it is advisable to bounce light off white or near-white surfaces. For example, if your ceiling is red, then light bounced off of it will have a reddish tinge. In this case, either a large bed sheet or white paper or the silvered side of a space blanket (available in camping supply stores) should be taped to the ceiling and the light bounced off of its surface (see Setting Up Shots).

To check how your lighting techniques will work in the final picture, set up the lights and then view the setting through the camera with the preview button depressed. The best gadget for checking your lighting setup is a Spectra Viewing Glass for color or black-and-white. If the arrangement does not seem right, then move the lights and look again. You may need to add or remove lights or to set small reflecting cards around the glass in order to get the right lighting but keep checking the scene through your camera's lens until you are satisfied.

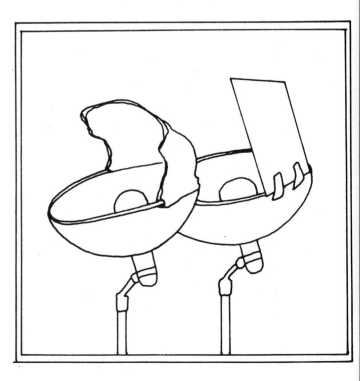

Neutral Backdrops

Neutral backdrops—such as photographer's no-seam, large sheets of paper, solid-colored bed sheets, and any other material that can be used as a backdrop—work very well for shooting lamps, lighted sculpture, and free-standing light boxes. However, there is nothing more sterile or plastic-like than a photograph of a window or panel meant for natural daylight, shot in artificial light against a neutral backdrop. The explanation for this disparity is directly related to the types of glass used for the two types of glasswork. Lamps, lighted sculpture, and similar constructions are generally cut from opalescent glass that has a great deal of character within the glass itself. Placing a neutral backdrop behind a lighted sculpture has no affect on how the glass appears but can eliminate a distracting background. Windows and panels meant for daylight are usually cut from antique glass that contains subtle striations, bubbles, and imperfections that only show up under certain lighting conditions. Antique glass relies upon light changes and the scenery behind the glass reflecting and blocking light to bring out its character. The minute you place a solid background behind antique glass, it appears to be plastic instead of glass. Try this experiment. Hold a piece of brilliant antique glass up to a bright white wall. Then hold it up to a window. In the first situation the glass will be dull and flat; in the second position it will appear full of life.

Color Film

At first glance, understanding the differences between color films might seem a bit baffling. There are two forms of color film—slides (transparencies) and prints (color negatives)—that can be purchased for either tungsten light or daylight to handle the three lighting conditions—fluorescent, tungsten, and daylight. To further complicate matters each film has a different ASA rating (film speed). The most professional way to deal with the whole affair is to try different films, filters, and techniques until you find your preferences and then stick with what you discover. Most photographers have their supplies down to just those few films that directly relate to their type of shooting, making it possible to forecast results.

Kodak films have been used for examples throughout these explanations because Eastman Kodak Corp. is generally accepted as a leader in the field and their films are the most widely distributed. Some films are presently being phased out and others are being introduced to take their place. The new films have two classifications, amateur and professional. The professional films might not be stocked by all film stores. All of the new films have two advantages over the films they replace. They are less polluting and are so easy to process that they can be handled at home or processed through a lab in just a few hours.

Amateur films can be mistreated in the usual ways: left in the camera for a few days, not processed immediately, etc. The professional films are far more sensitive. They are like ripe tomatoes and any minor negligence will ruin their precise, critical tolerances. The professional films are shipped to the camera store in refrigerated cars, where they are in turn stored in a refrigerator. After you have purchased the film, it requires an hour to thaw out, then it must be exposed and processed within the same twenty-four period. If you cannot have it processed within that time, it must be taken from the camera, put back in its plastic container, and stored in your refrigerator until the very first moment it can be processed. This type of film was developed for the working photographer. Until this new development, color films were always "cooking," that is, the emulsions were constantly maturing. The manufacturer had to estimate the amount of time that elapsed between manufacture, shipping, sitting on the camera store's shelf, and sitting in your camera for the film to reach its ideal state. The emulsions are usually close to the ideal by the time you shoot the film, but this kind of guesswork was never satisfactory for the professional. Ergo, the new professional films are sold to you at their exact point of perfection. If you tend towards being a perfectionist, in the best sense of the word, the quality difference is worth the extra trouble.

Slides are wonderfully versatile. They can be turned into color prints, duplicate slides, or black-and-white prints without a great loss in quality. They are the cheapest way to shoot in color and the accepted way to submit work for reproduction in magazines and books and for competition and exhibition. Once you understand how to work with slide film, print film is easy to master, but the reverse is not true.

If after considering all of the advantages, you still prefer to work with print film, then you should experiment with the new Kodacolor 400 ASA film. It is truly exceptional in its ability to handle almost any lighting condition without needing filters, and its high ASA rating is a lifesaver when working without a tripod. The other print films will give you fine colors when used in daylight but they must generally be used with a tripod and definitely require filtering for tungsten and fluorescent lights.

Bracketing

Bracketing is a standard procedure with photographers because the small variables, personal or mechanical error, processing, specific preferences, and needs often demand more than a single shot to do the job well.

Bracketing is really the art of hedging your bets. It is an automatic, professional way of making sure that you get the shot you want. Imagine this scene: The lighting is right; the correct film is loaded; the proper aperture is set; the meter reading has been taken; the speed is set; and the camera is mounted on the tripod, ready for the shot. At this point, instead of taking a single shot, take at least five shots without moving your camera or any other part of the camera except the aperture ring (F/stop ring). There is really no one perfect exposure, especially with glass. One of the five shots will be perfect for reproduction, another for projection, and still another for prints. It is well worth the minor cost of a few extra shots to make sure that you get what you want. To have saved a few cents and seconds and wasted your time in the end is a most depressing result, especially if you cannot reshoot the glass at a later date.

The first shot is chosen by setting your aperture and then taking a meter reading for speed. The other four shots are 1/2 stops away from the ideal in both directions. Take the first shot, then move the aperture ring one-half of the way towards the next full aperture, i.e., from F/5.6 towards F/4. Take the shot, move the aperture another 1/2 stop, and you'll be at F/4. Move the ring in the opposite direction until you are one-half of the way between F/5.6 and the next full aperture, F/8, and proceed as above to F/8. An even finer division for bracketing would be to bracket every 1/3 stop in both directions. In this case you would have seven instead of five shots for each new framing (fig. 4-9).

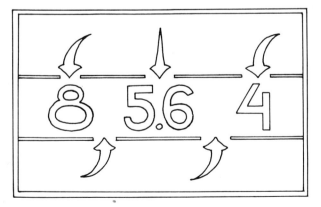

4-9. Arrows indicate where to set the lens in order to take five bracketed shots.

To bracket shots with an electronic camera, it must be set on manual. An electronic camera can be tricked into bracketing while still set on automatic but these techniques change with each model. Check with your camera store for the appropriate technique for your make of camera.

Tungsten Lighting

As mentioned earlier under Lighting, tungsten film must be shot with 3200°K bulbs for the truest color rendition. The minute you know that you are going to be shooting under tungsten lighting, think extra lights, neutral backdrops, crumpled sheets of aluminum foil or white bristol board for reflecting light, and at least one roll of 36-exposure film per object. In the end you can expect at least one really good shot and if you are lucky, three. The rule of thumb for all shootings is one shot per roll that really satisfies.

Tungsten Films	ASA
Slides	
Kodak Ektachrome 50 professional	50
Kodak Ektachrome 160 amateur or professional	160

Note: There are no 35mm print films made exclusively for tungsten light.

Daylight

If you wish to add light either in the interior or exterior of the room, then you must use a light source that is balanced between 5000–5800°K to match daylight film. Blue floodlights, blue tinted flash, or electronic flash can all be used. Blue floods are the cheapest and easiest to use of the three and are, therefore, the recommended choice for the newly initiated photographer. If you are shooting a window lighted by daylight, make sure to turn off all other house lights or replace them with blue floodlights; otherwise, the color balance of the film will be adversely affected.

Daylight Films	
Slides	ASA
Kodachrome 25	25
Kodachrome 64	64
Kodak Ektachrome 64 amateur or professional	64
Kodak Ektachrome 200 amateur or professional	200
Kodak Ektachrome 400 amateur	400

Prints	ASA
Kodacolor II	100
Kodacolor 400	400

Fluorescent Lighting

Since there is no film specifically designed for fluorescent lighting, you must use filters over the camera's lens and shoot with either tungsten or daylight film. There are a few different ways to mount these filters over your lenses, and the cheapest method is to buy a spring-loaded filter holder and gelatin filters. This type of holder will accommodate most lenses, but if you have a favorite lens that you use for most of your shootings, it's a good idea to check that the holder will work with that lens.

There are a few different types of fluorescent lamps: daylight, white, warm white, etc. The type of light is always printed on the sides of the lamp. Each kind of lamp requires a filter or filters. All filters are coded, for example, CC20Y. The CC stands for color compensating; the 20 stands for a density of 0.20 resistance to blue; and the Y stands for yellow. The full range of colors that you will be mixing are: M=magenta, Y=yellow, C=cyan and B=blue. Never use more than three filters at one time. The information on increasing stops pertains to only those cameras that do not have through-the-lens metering.

Type of Fluorescent Lamp	Type of KODAK Film	
	Daylight Film	Tungsten Film
Daylight	40M+30Y+1 stop	85B+30M+10Y +1 2/3 stops
White	20C+30M+1 stop	40M+40Y+1 stop
Warm White	40C+40M+ 1 1/3 stops	30M+20Y+1 stop
Warm White DeLux	60C+30M+ 1 2/3 stops	10Y+1/3 stop
Cool white	30M+2/3 stop	50M+60Y+ 1 1/3 stops
Cool White DeLux	20C+20M+1 stop	10M+30Y+2/3 stop

If you're in a bind and do not have CC filters in your camera bag, then shoot with any daylight film.

Color Prints

Many factors affect a color print, but generally you'll have more quality control working with a professional color lab in your area rather than with a mail-order firm. It costs slightly more to use a lab but certain services are available that would not be possible through mail order. Three such advantages are: You can work directly with a technician, request a clip test, and include a color chart for the lab to follow. A clip test means that the lab processes the first five or six shots but holds the rest until after you have approved the test strip. Since the lab has no way of knowing where they will cut the strip from the roll, you will probably lose a shot, but that is compensated for by bracketing.

When you and the technician examine the clip test, the actual glass will not be present for comparison so you will need some other standard by which to judge, e.g., a Kodak color chart. This chart comes with every Kodak Data Guide, and the Guide is basic equipment for nearly every professional photographer and lab.

By including the color chart in the first five or seven bracketed exposures, the lab will be able to check color accuracy and make adjustments, both during the developing process and by filtering during the printing process. For example, if you shot a single lamp on a roll of 36-exposure slide film, the first five bracketed shots would show the lamp plus the color chart below it, the next five bracketed exposures would be from a different position without the chart, and so on until you had shots of the lamp from seven different positions (35 exposures) with one exposure to spare. Then, when you want to have a print made, you need to take only two slides to the lab, one that includes the color chart and the one that you want to have printed. In the eventuality that the slide you want printed is the one with the color chart, the lab can crop out the chart during the printing.

Types of Prints

The four methods of making prints are called Ciabachrome, Type R, Type C, and Dye Transfer. For all practical purposes, Ciabachrome printing is a home darkroom process whereby you make a print directly from a slide (direct positive printing). If you have your own darkroom, it is definitely worth investigating this process since it is a relatively easy and inexpensive (albeit amateur) method of printing. The other three methods are usually handled through labs.

Type R prints are inexpensive, readily available, and unstable. They tend to fade more quickly than Type C or Dye Transfer prints and cannot be laminated. This process is the same as Ciabachrome in that it is a direct positive made from a transparency.

Type C prints are made directly from print (negative) films or from slides, using an inter-negative. This is a fine quality print, only a bit more expensive than Ciabachrome or Type R prints. Depending upon your original slide, the inter-negative used to make the final print will often improve the color quality. Type C prints can be laminated and used in presentation books and are suitable for lectures, etc.

Dye Transfer printing is literally the finest print money can buy. Unfortunately the cost is astronomical and only a rare occasion could justify the expense. With this type of printing process, total control of color value is available to the photographer since the colors are laid down in a manner that resembles silk-screen printing. If a color is meant to be blue, it can be any shade of blue or changed to a different color altogether.

You should know what you are getting from the lab. Always question which process they will use since they might use any or all of the three most common methods (Ciabachrome, Type R, or Type C). Dye Transfer is never considered unless you specifically request the process, and then cost will certainly be discussed. Unless the lab can give you specific reasons why a particular slide should not be printed by Type C, this is the best method to request.

Trouble Shooting
Conversion Filters

It may someday happen that you have the wrong type of film in your camera bag to take an important shot. The solution (if all the stores are closed) is to keep two glass filters on hand, an 85B and an 80A, that fit your favorite lens. These filters convert the way film sees light; tungsten film can be shot in daylight and daylight film can be shot in tungsten light. Covenient as this may sound, it is nevertheless an emergency measure. Quality is adversely affected, and it is always best to use the right film for the specific light.

Whenever you employ either filter, the effective A.S.A. rating of the film is considerably lowered. This is not much of a problem if your camera has through-the-lens metering and you are working with a fairly fast film. When you are using a hand-held meter, change the ASA speed rating on the light meter and leave it at the new setting as long as you are using the conversion filter.

Daylight Slide Films	Original ASA	New ASA in tungsten light with 80A filter
Kodachrome 25	25	6
Kodachrome 64	64	16
Kodak Ektachrome 64 amateur or professional	64	16
Kodak Ektachrome 200 amateur or professional	200	50
Kodak Ektachrome 400 amateur	400	100

Tungsten Slide Films	Original ASA	New ASA in daylight with 85B filter
Kodak Ektachrome 50 professional	50	32
Kodak Ektachrome 160 amateur or professional	160	100

Daylight Print Film	Original ASA	New ASA in tungsten light with 80A filter
Kodacolor II	100	25
Kodacolor 400	400	100

Record Keeping with Black-and-White Film

It seems obvious to shoot stained glass with color film. While the life expectancy of most color films is excellent, it is important to be aware that dyes will fade in time. The rate and amount of fading is affected by storage temperature and humidity and to the amount and type of light to which the prints or slides are subjected. If long life of color photographs is part of your thinking, then special care is needed for handling and storing color materials.

Black-and-white film has a much longer lifetime as evidenced by the big market in old prints. If you want pictures to show your great-grandchildren, shoot everything that is important in both color and black-and-white film. For the finest grain, use a very slow film such as Kodak Panatomic-X film. This will provide the sharpest results; however, a tripod (and possibly extra lights) is an absolute necessity with this film.

Polarizing Filter

This filter removes reflected glare from the sun or interior floodlights and is very simple to operate. Simply by rotating the filter, glare disappears. It allows you to take reflection-free shots of glass sculpture outdoors and is a great help whenever you have the problem of light bouncing off of rather than penetrating the glass surface. Another use for this filter is to add color saturation to your photographs.

Pushing

Pushing is the technique of increasing the speed of a film by exposing it at a faster ASA than rated and having it specially processed. This is accomplished by changing the ASA on your light meter no more than two stops. For example, if the film is rated for ASA 160, one stop would push it to 320; two stops would push it to 640, in other words, doubling the ASA for each stop pushed. The films that are pushed in this progression are: Kodak Ektachrome 160 and 200 and 400. Kodak Tri-X film is pushed with a different progression: 400, 800, 1200, and 1600. Tri-X and the Ektachrome films are the only films that Kodak recommends pushing. They also do not recommend pushing film over 2 stops; however, it can be done with varying results. Pushing film is very helpful when you do not have a tripod and the light level is too low to shoot without one. It will also increase your contrast.

Presentations
Presentation Books

Putting together a presentation book is superfluous to stained glass work unless you decide to turn your hobby into a profession. Friends who have watched your art grow and develop need little more than an enthusiastic description to grasp the imagery of a proposed work. On the other hand, the person who would commission you to do a piece for a library, school, bank, or other public building would have no such advantage. You can be assured that any major expenditure on their part would be up for open bid with different artists submitting work for appraisal and comparison. You might be expected to produce a slick-looking presentation book and a formal contract proposal that encompassed such details as who would handle installation, how much it would cost, and when it would take place. For a large commission, a full-scale architectural model is also very helpful.

All this may lie somewhere in your future but for now a less grandiose book geared to smaller commissions would be a definite advantage to your commercial enterprises. Gather together all of your favorite photographs of your best work and have them enlarged to 5-by-7-inch or 8-by-10-inch (12.7 × 17.8cm or 20.3 × 25.4cm) glossy color prints. If a particular piece requires more than one shot to do it justice, then include as many as necessary. Arrange the shots in logical groupings and mount them between the plastic pages of a leather presentation book. These books are available through most large stationery or art stores. Special adhesive for color prints is available through art and camera supply stores. Other examples of your work that could be included are color renditions of a piece of work and the photograph of the end results, or a sample of lesser works in slide form, mounted in plastic pages that hold twenty slides per page.

A more sophisticated presentation book could be made with an expensive-looking, large-size, leather attaché case filled with individually mounted 8-by-10-inch (12.7 × 17.8cm) slides. Any good color lab can enlarge a 35mm slide to 8-by-10-inches and you can mount them on your own. To mount them, cut out two window frames from a sturdy black cardboard, then sandwich the slide plus two protective pieces of plastic between the window frames (fig. 4–10). When finished, the oversized transparency will have to be held up to the light to be seen, and the viewer will be treated to a very realistic image of light passing through glass.

Another idea for a presentation that works very well at craft shows, where an unprotected photograph would be handled to death is to laminate color prints. Have your color lab enlarge the photographs to 8-by-10-inches (12.7 × 17.8cm) by the Type C printing process and then have the prints laminated onto stiff cardboard. The lamination will be similar to the luster of real glass.

4-10.   Sandwiching an 8″ × 10″ (20.32cm × 25.4 cm) slide.

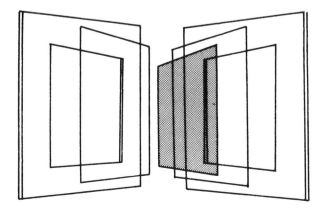

Proposals

If your book lands you a commission, then you should make a color mock-up of the proposed work and fix a fair price for your work with an ample margin for increased prices and unforeseen costs. This is called a proposal.

A variety of materials can be used to make a mock-up of a project; including watercolor, casein, colored pencil, colored paper, paint on acetate, and press-on colors. The drawing or collage should resemble the finished work as closely as possible.

Start with something uncomplicated such as colored pencils on heavy velum tracing paper with inked-in lead lines. Mount the drawing on shiny white cardboard and cover with acetate. By mounting the drawing on white cardboard, you will have created a reflective surface, while the protective acetate covering gives the feeling of glass. As you become more at ease with making proposals, you can investigate other construction methods.

Pricing Your Work

It's difficult to price your own work when you are starting out because it is most probably a totally new experience. There is a definite tendency to underprice or, at best, just to "break even." To overcome this inclination, you must keep accurate records of the cost of materials and time spent on a job. Never commit yourself to a large commission without thoroughly considering the cost in terms of time and materials, or you may end up paying for it yourself.

Estimate generously for all materials and base your costs on current retail prices. It is misleading to use a local studio's pricing as a guide; as an individual artist you are denied the considerable discounts and advantages that are available to them. Figure that you will need double the quantity of glass for each color in a design to allow for excessive breakage. To figure out your hourly wage, you should charge what you would pay someone else to do the job, hopefully somewhere above the minimum working wage per hour. Add this to the estimated cost of all materials and the total is what you should charge. In the end, the biggest problem is often finding enough courage to ask for your price.

These guidlines should prove fairly accurate until such time as when your work becomes very popular and in demand; then, what the heck, hire an agent.

INDEX